# DIARY
# INNOVATOR
## *Finding the Path Not Taken*

# *T O M   B O R G E R*

# Praise | Diary of an Innovator

⊙ "Tom's experience as an innovator, entrepreneur, and advisor allows him to impart actionable (and entertaining!) stories that would-be innovators and leaders can use to achieve meaningful outcomes. Tom brings an undying optimism that anything is possible and palpable energy to a topic that is too often dry and academic. Among the volumes that have been written on innovation, this one is worth reading!"
**~ Roy Rosin—Former Chief Innovative Officer, Intuit, Chief Innovative Officer University of Pennsylvania Health System**

⊙ "Tom's first person account makes this a unique and very interesting book about innovation. It is the story telling itself and his relentless desire to learn from every experience that makes the book compelling. It is a textbook for business school students albeit one that is quite breezy and readable. It is also an insider's guide to what it really takes to be an entrepreneur inside a company." **~ Michael Sneed— Vice President, Global Corporate Affairs, Johnson & Johnson**

⊙ "Tom Borger's **Diary of an Innovator** captures the essence of the struggle that exists between innovators and the status quo in organizations. His stories are insightful and entertaining. Tom delivers his message in an easy and conversational tone. It is a highly enjoyable read."
**~ Ian McPherson—Former President, GSK Consumer International**

⊙ "Tom's passion and optimism about the possibilities and potential of innovation in large organizations comes to life in this easy-to-read narrative. You can't help but feel energized about "what can be" versus "what is" after you read the book.

Tom is a great role model for all of us and this book is a must read!" ~ **Walter Buckley—Chairman and CEO, Internet Capital Group**

⊙ "Tom is an expert in innovation. Not because he has studied it, but because he has done the hard work of actually driving innovation in environments as varied as startup companies and fortune 100 corporations. Oh yeah, he also tells wild and entertaining stories."
~ **Brad Aronson—Former President of i-Frontier**

⊙ "Tom has an outstanding track record of driving innovation in many different business, academic and personal settings. He has a unique ability to do it, teach, preach it and most importantly get others to be better at it. There hasn't been a conversation I've had with him where I don't feel challenged, energized and motivated. Many talk it, he lives it."
~ **Peter Luther—President, J&J Consumer**

⊙ "When I think innovation I think of Tom Borger. This book will help those of you who want to be innovative but just haven't figured out where to start. Along the way you will get to know Tom and his family through clever storytelling and beautiful moments. This is one business book that is not only helpful, but it will also make you smile."
~ **Joe Payne—former CEO, Eloqua**

⊙ "**Diary of an Innovator** is an excellent tool for anyone looking to start a new business. It provides the stimulus to really look at things different, and then to go and do it. This book shows that innovation is when mindset meets action. Innovation is a sport of the mind and the body, and Tom is an excellent coach. His book gives you a great game plan to up your game. If you are looking to enter the Big Leagues of innovation - whether within your company or starting your own business - read this book. It's time to get off the bench!"
~ **Steve Luttmann— CEO, Leblon**

⊙  "An innovative book by a true innovator! Tom does a great job of crafting an insightful book on what it takes to enact change, whether in one's personal life or professional life. He has distilled the lessons learned and observations made during his evolving career as an innovator, teacher, coach and father into a compelling and enjoyable read."

**~ Ashesh Shah—CEO, Maxx Orthopedics**

⊙  "As readers of this book will quickly learn, Tom is a unique combination of innovator and motivator. His ideas and vision have helped companies at various stages identify where innovation can catalyze business evolution, despite the predictable barriers to change. Powered by Tom's energy and art for storytelling, [this book] is an enjoyable ride that delivers a plan for action."  **~ Steve Wray—CEO, Cadient**

⊙  "If you are lucky, you find a few people in your life for whom you make time, no matter how busy you may be. One of those people for me is Tom Borger. I have known Tom for over 25 years when we began our careers together as Management Associates. While our careers have moved in different directions, we have stayed in touch over the decades. Every conversation with Tom reconnects me to the promise of possibility. We are kindred spirits who realize that every obstacle is an opportunity and every resistor is a possible co-creator. Tom has a profound *joie de vivre* that is evident in all his worldly roles: author, entrepreneur, teacher, husband, father, and friend. Tom's book may be directed to the business community, but I have it on my daughter's reading list."

**~ Julie McHugh—Former Company Group Chairman, J&J, Former CEO, Nora Therapeutics, Former President, Centocor, Inc, and Current Director on Viropharma, Inc. Board of Directors**

⊙  "Tom provides a series of lessons learned through numerous entertaining stories about innovation. The book is a compilation of short stories on innovation that provide valuable insights for leaders, entrepreneurs and anyone who wants to

make a difference.  It is an inspiration for people who want to try something that has not been done."        **~ Ron Hunt—**
**Managing Director of New Leaf Venture Partners**

⊙   "I have known Tom for 20 years.  He has a unique, remarkable ability to create possibility no matter what the issue or perceived obstacle.  This book shares his insights on human behavior, and how to see opportunity whether in business or life.   And, since Tom never takes himself too seriously, his book conveys a level of humility and humor that makes it really easy and fun to read.  Enjoy!"
**~ Bob Carpenter—President and CEO, GS1 U.S.**

⊙   "*Diary of an Innovator* is a user's guide to turn dreams into reality. Tom delivers entertaining stories that punctuate a common theme for innovation, observing, understanding and learning from failure is critical to overcome the hurdles on the path to success.  This is a must read for leaders tackling innovation initiatives."        *~ Steve Tullman—Managing Partner*
*NeXeption, Chairman & CEO Ceptaris Therapeutics, Chairman & Co-founder Aclaris Therapeutics, Prior President, CEO & Co-founder Ception Therapeutics, Prior Chairman & Co-founder Vicept Therapeutics, Prior CBO & Co-founder Trigenesis Therapeutics, Prior GlaxoSmithKline*

# Table of Contents

# Preface

I had a number of very kind friends and colleagues who subjected themselves to the early, unfiltered versions of this book. Special thanks to Brad Aronson and Michael Sneed who were the first to read the earliest (and ugliest) version of this book. I really appreciated the feedback and the inspiration! Their input was instrumental in getting this book finished. One common theme came up which I would like to address head on. Who is this book for? In the most basic marketing concept: who is the target audience? Despite all of my experience and training, I reluctantly report that there is not one "go to" target audience. I believe this book provides a number of different people with useful information. It is not all things to all people; it is different things to each person. I hope that comes through as you read it as there is something for everyone. A few of the audiences who I hope can benefit from many of my first-hand experiences with innovation include:

→ Innovation and corporate leaders—there are tons of lessons for leaders responsible for driving innovation and new value creation in large corporations
→ Innovators—countless examples of ways to overcome obstacles and hurdles that stand in the way of success
→ Entrepreneurs—whether you are "on your own" or inside a company there are words of reinforcement and empowerment to you
→ Business school students—there is so much to know…and so little time to learn. I hope I made it easy to learn some great lessons that will make you more valuable in whatever role you play.
→ Coaches—this may seem like an outlier, but there are

many, many lessons in the power of belief that apply to business (and sports) coaches

Another point of feedback on the book had to do with the inclusion of some stories (e.g. stand-up comedy experience in high school) that did not include an obvious innovative solution. I share these stories in an attempt to help give you the mindset—or the DNA component—of innovators. There were many events that helped give shape to the innovations I pursued. The characteristics that helped me carry through those innovations were hard-coded or at least strongly influenced by some of these events and experiences. I felt it was important to provide you with that additional dimension as it may help you reflect on your own foundational experiences that may shape your future drive for success.

It is my hope and desire that everyone who reads my book can get something out of it that is useful for them...and can have a laugh along the way to learning. Most importantly, I want this book to be more than "thought-provoking." I want it to be "action-provoking," because thinking isn't doing...doing is doing!

Special thanks to my talented artist-of-a-sister, Julie Ferguson, who patiently and painstakingly worked with me to create the cover artwork!

Finally, I want to thank my kids, Mia, Luke, Quinn and Brynn for providing continual inspiration to me every day and for reminding me that everything is easier through the eyes of children. They did not see the obstacles... just the opportunities.

Finally, finally, I want to thank my wife Anita who has been incredibly supportive. Her comments and editing were a huge, huge help in making this a reality.

# Why I Wrote This Book

**Reason 1: I always think there is a better way.**
I have always been someone who is easily annoyed, flustered and somewhat frustrated when I see something done differently than I would have done it. I could just "chill out" and not think much more about it, but that's not the way I am wired. Those pesky frustrations and annoyances are the source of opportunity and this motivates me to action.

**Reason 2: Making roads is more fun than traveling down roads that are already built.**
I have also been someone who quite enjoys clearing a path down the road not traveled at all, or making my own roads. There is not a famous poem about this one because Robert Frost failed to recognize that there were actually three paths. "Two roads diverged in a yellow wood"—this much we know from Frost. But the third "road" was not a path at all. It was waiting to become one! It's more fun to do what has not been done before than to do something the way others have—at least in my eyes.

**Reason 3: I believe that anything is possible.**
I have undying optimism. In my personal life, this characteristic is refreshing and uplifting (as far as I know!). In a business context, this is often dismissed as naivety. You can, in fact, do almost anything if you want it bad enough and are willing to work hard enough for it. Optimism is a huge asset when it comes to innovation. The reason is simple. Most people believe that if it were possible, and if it were in fact a legitimate opportunity, it would already have been done. That leaves a

huge amount of opportunity for those fearless enough to get things done. That reminds me of the quote from Charles H. Duell, the Commissioner of US patent office in 1899 who famously stated that "everything that can be invented has been invented." This was not the most uplifting message to budding entrepreneurs—especially considering that it came from the person with the responsibility to provide patent protection on new ideas. Fortunately, his comments did not stop (or even slow) the entrepreneurs and innovators. More than 7 million patents have been issued since his bold proclamation of 1899...and counting!

**Reason 4: I want my kids to make a career out of their passion.**
At the ripe old age of 48, I have accumulated a fair amount of wisdom (read: made a lot of mistakes) that I would like to impart. I am hoping that I first impart to you the reader (as well as to my kids) that you must find a way to make your passion your job.

I grew up being told—and mostly believing—that things you loved doing may be fun but you could not make a living doing those things. They could be hobbies or things you love to do to pass the time, but at some point, you had to "get serious," "be practical," and focus on building skills that you could use as a foundation for a career in something other than what you love doing. How horrible is that? Pretty horrible, AND completely false!

Have you ever wondered how people who have really cool jobs got them? They had the courage to follow their passion. On a recent family vacation to Jamaica, I ran into a young dive master who was teaching SCUBA lessons in the hotel pool. He told me his plans to travel the globe, continue with higher levels of certification and teach SCUBA everywhere he goes. He was young and he made his passion his job. His "job" allowed him to see the world and do exactly what he loves doing. For me, I love teaching. That is why I teach at Wharton's Small Business Development Center and Villanova's School of Business and it is why I am writing a book on innovation. I hope that this book will help me teach people that I would otherwise not be able to reach. I must also admit that I LOVE being on stage—presenting to audiences, and this book is a platform to allow me to do more of that in the future.

My "learned wisdom" that I now freely pass along to anyone that will listen is this: "Focus on the intersection of what you love doing and what you are really good at doing." Make your passion your job.

**Reason 5: Challenge big company executives to manage the strengths of their talent rather than focus on improving their weaknesses.**
This is the only way to harness the talent of your people. I've worked for a number of big companies that take really talented and motivated people with "gifts" or skills in different areas and turn them into average and unhappy employees. How is this possible? Human Resource departments believe that you need to identify "opportunity areas" or weaknesses with employees and then provide them with training to rehabilitate or improve those areas. On the contrary, I believe you should focus on the "gifts" your employees possess and tap into their passion for the things that they love <u>and</u> are good at doing. Create opportunities for them to unleash their passion as a catalyst for your business. Focus on the strength of your people not their weakness.

**Reason 6: Individuals are what drive culture.**
Many people believe that culture determines whether they can be innovative. Some will lament that if they were only in a culture that is more conducive to innovation, then they would, in fact, innovate. This is the "I would if I could" syndrome which

afflicts some with a feeling of helplessness and resignation. In essence, these individuals are abdicating responsibility and accountability for creating new value to an abstract entity called "culture" that has no emotion (heart) or intelligence (brain). Culture is not a person. It can't think nor can it act. Culture only exists because of the collective learning of all of the individuals in a business, function or team. Individuals have all of the power. If they do not like the perceived culture, they have to realize that as an individual contributing to the culture, they have the ability to affect it. Culture is often an excuse for inaction by people who lack the passion and will to take action themselves. In truth, individuals, not the culture, determine all action.

**Reason 7: There are no good business books that make it fun to learn stuff.**
My writing style is light, whimsical, and filled with fun stories, numerous asides and random movie references. I believe that really good learning comes only with a mixture of good content (stories and lessons in this case) delivered in an entertaining way. I have been accused at various points in my life (and business career) of not taking things seriously enough. Guilty as charged, but my retort was always the same: You can get just as much work done with a smile on your face as you can with a scowl. Choose positivity and "can do." Life is too short not to enjoy. It is a choice...your choice.

**Reason 8: People who say "no," simply do not "know."**
This is a critical principal. When you and your idea first get rejected with a resounding "no," how should you respond? I believe you need to hear "know" instead of "no." What I mean by that is the person who says "no" clearly does not "know" what you know, because if they did, they would say "yes." This is an empowering principal as it forces the entrepreneur/innovator to maintain control of the process of driving for new value. You need to take "no" as a signal that you have more

work to do. It is not their fault for not knowing, it is your fault for not letting them know. You are always in control and never a victim.

**Reason 9: There is no such thing as bad news...just new information.**
Bad news is crippling and can stop you in your tracks. New information creates an opportunity for you to learn where the right path is. It allows you to adapt in order to succeed. New information is simply something that you learn that you did not know before. It was true before you learned it, but until you learned it, you simply did not know that you were heading down the wrong path. Now that you know, you can pivot to the right path to success. You need to be thankful for "new information" as that is how you "course correct" your way to success.

**Reason 10: I have the attention span of a gnat.**
I wrote this book the way I did because I am so easily bored with books—particularly business books—that drone on and on and never seem to deliver the final learning I am seeking. I have broken this book into bite-sized nuggets of knowledge. I hope that I accomplish these three things with each story: good content, entertaining delivery, lessons that you can apply to your world—business, community and family. Please feel free to give me your feedback at: **feedback@diaryofaninnovator.com**.

**Reason 11: Having 10 reasons just seems too conformist for an author of a book on innovation (I'm just being honest).**

Kidding aside, the 11$^{th}$ reason is that I have always wanted to write a book. I wrote a lot of poetry in high school and college as a way of organizing my thoughts and providing an outlet for my passion on various subjects. I kept writing "stuff" in college with the intent of writing an amusing book about the transition from the "un-real" world of college to the "real world" of work. It has taken me a while and there have been some pretty monumental thematic shifts to the story, but I am finally getting around to finishing the project. Here it is! I hope you enjoy it.

# 1 | Quinn the Innovator: Don't Let Experience Blind You to Opportunities!

Kids are the greatest teachers. I have four children who teach me something new every day. One particularly memorable lesson occurred on a beautiful spring afternoon on my back patio with my 6-year-old daughter, Brynn and my 9-year-old son, Quinn. Brynn was having a grand old time creating bubbles by dipping a "wand" of sorts into a small bowl of liquid soap/bubble formula. She was quite amused with all of the bubbles she was making and was also quite territorial with her implements of amusement. Quinn wanted "in" on the action and Brynn wanted nothing to do with Quinn's "action." Quinn tried a number of ways to try to coax the wand out of Brynn's hand. Finding no success through these traditional and polite means, he eventually resorted to stealing it outright. That is when I had to intercede on my daughter's behalf.

After more discussion than should have been required to get the wand back into my daughter's hands, I finally told Quinn to leave his sister alone and go find something else to do. Quinn wandered thoughtfully (more accurately, he stormed off) around the side of the house and went into the garage. I heard a bunch of strange banging and clanging noises from items that were apparently either tossed or knocked over in the garage. There was so much banging and clanging coming from the garage, it sounded like he was trying to build a car out of scrap metal. Ever the curious one, I decided to wander over to see what all of the commotion was about. I walked around the side of the house and peered into the garage. There, I saw Quinn bent over, rustling through a number of things in the garage before he finally emerged from a pile of "stuff" with his sought after prey in his hands. He turned to me triumphantly and displayed a giant bucket and a huge container of the liquid soap/bubbles. I just kept wondering, "What is he up to?"

As I looked at his smiling face, my eyes were quickly drawn to something on the floor of the garage just past where he was standing and then my "experience" began to kick in. "Wait a minute! Hold on! Whatever you are planning to do, NO, you can't do it." That was me, dear old dad "the innovative buzz saw" cutting off my son's self-made innovation plans in one fell swoop. I had no idea what Quinn was planning to do, but I did see a gigantic mess on the floor of the garage that was produced by one of the things that he was planning to use in his plan. I logically concluded that any combination of the aforementioned "bubble solution" with anything else would likely lead to a similar mess.

The mess itself was a giant amoeba-like stain. It reminded me of the outline of bodies that you sometimes see on TV shows where police outline the body of the deceased with chalk on the ground. The origin of the stain is actually a funny story. That same big ol' container of bubble solutions (which is a type of liquid soap) had been in the garage for awhile—though not always in a strictly vertical position (that would have been way to confining). At some point, the container tipped over, and rested on its side. The lid, it would appear, must not have been tightly sealed as some of the liquid soap slowly seeped out onto the floor of the garage. This Valdez-like bubble spill probably went on for a few days (maybe even weeks) and grew quite large before anyone either recognized it for what it was, or decided that it was enough of a nuisance that they would take some action to clean it up. Apparently, the mess did not reach the tipping point where someone would actually feel compelled to take an action like pick up the bottle, tighten the lid, or mop up the mess. That would be far too much to expect, right? Remember, kids are not burdened by experience so they didn't see the mess as a mess.

Now... here is the funny part. It's liquid soap, right? You use soap to clean things, right? Well, you'd think that something that is designed to clean dirt would somehow have built up some level of resistance to dirt as well. This, in fact, is not the case. When this gooey soap is confronted with it's natural enemy, dirt, it somehow takes on some very strange "fatal attraction-like" characteristics. The dirt and soap combine to form a sort of "super dirt" that is impervious to any and all efforts to clean it up. The super dirt seemed to attract from far and wide, every bit of dirt, dust, pollen, small bugs, and random pieces of floating garbage. This toxic mixture solidified itself into a cement-like varnish that is like a permanent "tattoo" adorning the garage floor as we speak.

OK, so maybe I'm exaggerating a little bit, but you get the point. I could not escape my past experience. I had seen this movie before and I knew the ending—it ends with a super dirt mess that could endanger the world! This would then be followed by numerous futile attempts to eliminate the super dirt. I thought, "No, Quinn...whatever it is you are planning, I'm pretty sure the answer is no. I've seen the future and the future is a mess!"

So there was my boy, excited as can be about his idea. And there I was—a supervisor of sorts—ready to squash his idea (even before I knew what it was) and his enthusiasm like a little bug because I could not see past the mess. Surely, I thought, "Nothing good could come of this effort—whatever it might be." I was so smart and experienced that I knew better. Still, I asked for (OK maybe "demanded" is more in line with the tone I had) an explanation for what he intended to do.

Quinn quietly explained to me that all he was trying to do was to make a "really big bubble." I thought to myself how cute his comments were... and then told him, knowingly, "Quinn, the size of the bucket does not make the bubble any bigger." He looked at me a little surprised and said, "I know dad, but I need a big space to start." And then he reached in his pocket and pulled out a really long shoelace, and quickly added, "I'm going to tie the ends of this long shoe-lace together and create a really big circle, and then I'm going to dip it into the bucket, lift it out and pull it against the wind to make a really big bubble." I think he may have even uttered a barely audible "duh" after his explanation to me as I clearly did not see what was so obvious to him.

"Now that is a hell of a thing," I thought to myself. I was dumbfounded. It was brilliant. My boy was way out of the box. He saw things I could not see. He figured out everything he needed to perform his "rapid prototype." And he was ready to make it happen. And there I was, "Mr. Innovation," stonewalling him by saying "no" before I even knew what he was trying to do. All of my experience, all of the things I knew, were telling me that whatever he was going to try to do would fail and lead to a mess. I must admit that even though I was ready to change my tune and let him try, I still had my doubts. I believed that the bubble "sauce" would not bind completely to the shoelace. Also, his fingers would get in the way as he dipped the shoelace into the bucket of bubble solution and pulled it back out. There were a bunch of reasons I still believed that his idea would fail. But he believed. His belief ultimately won me over despite my doubts. I told him, "Go for it, Quinn! Not in the garage...do it on the grass out back so that there is no more mess in the garage."

And then it happened. He dipped in the big circle he made with his shoelace, pulled it up, and waived it gently in the air and formed a gigantic bubble—just the way that he had pictured it in his head. It was awesome! It was so simple to

him. He saw things I could not see. He saw success. He saw
fun. He saw possibility. He saw action. He made it happen.
The bubbles were huge, and more importantly, he was really,
really fired up about what he had created from nothing! My
son... the innovator... that has a nice ring to it!

While impressed with my son for his accomplishment, I was also
very reflective about my own actions as a leader. I almost
stopped him from trying because I was blinded by a mess that I
could not overlook. My own experience prevented me from
seeing the possibility of what could be a really cool innovative
solution. I then reflected on the implications of this learning to
the corporate world.

How many times in a corporate setting do experienced
executives play my role here? Executives, who do not fully
understand or appreciate what it is that their employees are
trying to do, prevent them from even trying because they have
seen the mess that was created in the past. Every situation is a
new opportunity to learn. You cannot be the one that shuts
down the creativity and passion of your people before they
even try. You must unleash them on your most critical business
challenges and encourage them to try "stuff." Make things
happen. They will not always be successful, but they will always
be looking for ways to make the business better...if you let
them.

I learned a lot about me, innovation and parenting that day
from my boy. Here is a link to a summary of this story on
YouTube: http://www.youtube.com/watch?v=EV9GyhmxLSs.

**Lessons learned from *Quinn the Innovator:  Don't Let Experience Blind You to Opportunities!***

⊙ **Experience can blind you to new opportunities**.  The more you know, the less you see.  The less you see, the less you do.  Also, the more you know, the less you allow others to try.  Just because something may not have worked in the past does not mean that it cannot work in the future—especially when there is a person who believes.

⊙ **Don't underestimate the power of inexperience as a driver of innovation.**  Often times, the best innovators get things done because they did not know that it was supposed to be impossible.  Quinn was not thinking of the ways that his bubble could not be created, he just believed he could do it... and he did.

⊙ **Listen**.  Make sure you know what someone is trying to do before you say "no."  Don't presume you know what others are trying to do.  Let them explain.  Every situation is new.  Every person brings different strengths to the table.

⊙ **You must let people follow their passion and try things— even if you don't think it is the right thing**.  Even when you think you have all the answers, you may just find a better one by letting people try it their way.

⊙ **As a leader, provide your people with a garage full of "stuff."**  Leave them alone and don't worry about the potential mess.  If there is no mess then there is no trying.  Innovation can be messy.

⊙ **Give people the freedom to make mistakes.**  It is the best way to learn and to teach people to be accountable for their actions.  There is no faster path to learning than doing.

⊙ **When you start saying "no" before you fully understand the situation...hit the re-set button!** You don't know it all and you can't do it all so let others try to make a difference. You think you know it all, but you don't. Let others try. You may just find a better way.

# 2 | Culture and the Corporate Antibodies That Protect It

I spent much of my early career playing Gnip-Gnop between two great companies (Johnson & Johnson and GlaxoSmithKline) with a brief but meaningful stint at P&G in-between. I also had the opportunity to start my own internet business (Omnichoice). I have accumulated quite a few stories of innovation over the years. I know what it takes to get it done in big companies and in start-ups. The lessons are universally applicable to anyone who has tried to drive innovation in a business. One constant for innovation is that it is not easy—particularly in large corporations. That said, once you understand that resistance is a natural reaction to innovation, it is easier to overcome the obstacles standing in the way of success.

All companies claim to want to drive more innovation and create a more innovative culture. So why can't they? Why do companies seem to resist the very thing that they desire: innovation? The truth of the matter is that there are no innovative companies. There are only innovative people at companies that create "innovative companies." That is a fact! The people make the company what it is, not the other way around. Companies don't innovate, people do. There are companies who attract innovative people, and those innovative people drive innovation at their respective companies. By themselves, companies cannot think nor can they take any action. People who work for companies can. In short, it is the people who do things. It is people who innovate. Companies do nothing.

Some company executives would argue that the critical ingredient to successful innovation is the process. While process is important, the people are the premium when it comes to driving innovation. You need to attract, retain, recognize and reward the sort of people who thrive in ambiguity and relish the challenge of solving problems and creating new value. Additionally, companies need to get the most out of the people they already have. This can be accomplished by assessing the strengths of individuals and allowing people to self-select into areas where they can apply their strengths to help drive new business value. Whether you are attracting the missing innovative ingredients by recruiting new talent into the company or maximizing the contributions of the people you already have, the key is that each person recognizes that they play a critical role in getting things done. This is what creates the culture of innovation in organizations.

I have conducted numerous innovation seminars and workshops at corporations and the culture of the organization is always the elephant in the room. It is the most oft-used excuse for inaction. A critical part of evolving the culture at companies is getting people at those companies to understand that the responsibility for the innovation and culture rests squarely with them. It is very similar to the lesson that Po, the lovable "Kung Fu Panda," learned in his quest for the sacred scroll. The scroll was rumored to provide the ultimate wisdom of the universe and it would give the bearer great power once it was in his/her possession. After a long and tumultuous journey, Po finally had the scroll in his hands. He anxiously rolled out the scroll to see the content that would change his world. To his surprise there were no words on the scroll. All that Po could see was his reflection in the scroll. That was the ultimate wisdom that provides great power. He had to realize that it was in him. That is the key to culture and innovation within companies. People need to realize that it is in them.

To highlight this point when I run innovation workshops, I like to conduct a small little interactive exercise with the participants. I have a large poster board with seven different "pairs" of innovation-related opposite characteristics, e.g. can't do vs. can do, slow vs. fast, low energy vs. high energy, etc. First, I ask people to take a sticky note and place it on the board in the place between the paired opposites that represents their view of where the <u>company</u> ranks on each continuum. This is always met with some backhanded swipes at the company and knowing glances from the participants who all believe that the company has a culture that is woefully short of where it needs to be to support the innovation cause. Sure enough, the views of the participants reflect a pretty low ranking on every scale included in the quick survey.

Then, I ask the participants to rank where <u>they</u> stand—as an individual—on those same characteristics. It is fascinating—though not altogether surprising—that there is always a huge gap between their perceptions of the business and themselves. The business is always worse than the individual. Or in a more positive light, the people are always better than the business. Most people size up the now completed response board and conclude that it represents a fair and reasonable view of the reality of where the company and individuals rank. The participants think that their work is done, but I don't let them off so easily.

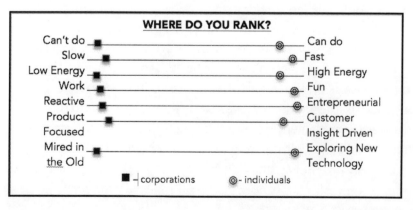

**WHERE DO YOU RANK?**

| | |
|---|---|
| Can't do | Can do |
| Slow | Fast |
| Low Energy | High Energy |
| Work | Fun |
| Reactive | Entrepreneurial |
| Product Focused | Customer Insight Driven |
| Mired in the Old | Exploring New Technology |

■ - corporations    ◎ - individuals

I burst their collective and individual bubbles by pointing out to them that, practically speaking, it is impossible for the individuals in a company to be significantly one way (more innovative) and the culture to be significantly the other way (less innovative). Culture is defined as the sum total of all learned behavior. The collection of all of the learned behavior of the individuals forms the culture. Every individual rates themselves on the more positive end of the innovation scale than the company. So if every individual contributing to the culture is more innovative than the culture…what gives? Either the participants were being overly harsh on the company or overly generous on their self-assessment. The culture should reflect the attitudes, beliefs and actions of the individuals in the organization. Culture is the sum of the experiences and learning of the individuals in the company. It can't be different than the collective experience of the individuals.

"Culture" tends to be the most often used excuse for lack of innovation in companies. What I try to communicate in my workshops is that no matter what you believe the culture to be, you are a contributor to, rather than a victim of, that culture. To quote one of my former managers, "control the controllable." You can control what you do, what you say, and how you react to what others do and say. You cannot control what others do or say. Focus on what you can control. This means that even in a company where the "culture" seems to be stacked against innovation, you can do what you can do. You and the individual members of your team can be a spark for innovation. And that effort can have a ripple effect on the evolution of the company culture as others learn from you. There is no culture without you (collectively, all of the individuals in the company). And you impact the culture more than it impacts you. Even when the culture impacts you, it is because you allow that to happen. You make the decision to do or not do something. Culture does not do that. Culture has no brain and cannot think and act for itself. Only individuals can think and act for themselves.  It seems hard to believe that an individual can change the culture of big companies but that is the only way that culture changes—through the efforts, attitudes and beliefs of the individuals.

So if it is not the culture that is preventing people from being more active change agents and innovators, what could it be?  I think it may have something to do with the aversion that most people have to stress.  Not many people would knowingly submit themselves to a more stressful environment if they had a choice.  While I am no psychologist, I did take a few psychology courses in my undergraduate days and one of the key surprises was the impact change has on stress.  The biggest surprise was that one of the most stressful events in life is marriage (which should only be a good thing, right?).  Yes, it is a good thing, but it does cause major league stress because it is a significant change in someone's life.  All change—even good change—causes stress.

So it should not be at all surprising that change in corporations creates stress.  What does this have to do with innovation? Well, any innovation is going to cause stress on people in the organization because something is being done differently than it had been done in the past.  It makes people very uncomfortable to deal with things in which they have neither the experience nor the expertise.  For lack of relevant experience, people will resort to the only experience they have and pretend it is relevant.  Unfortunately, this often causes people to lead with their fears instead of their hopes and desires.  Typically, people are more afraid of failure and the repercussions of that failure than they are excited about the prospect for success.

What does this innovation-induced stress trigger in people?  A reaction:  stress causes people to seek out and destroy the source of the stress.  They take out their vengeance on the new approach and the person behind the approach. This is what I affectionately refer to as the "corporate immune system" at work.

## Corporate Immune System

Like the body's own immune system, the corporate immune system is designed to protect the corporation from foreign matter. The company may be exposed to some toxin and the immune system recognizes the foreign matter and produces antibodies to go out and destroy it. The corporate antibodies are actually people who are focused on eliminating anything that does not look like the rest of the organization (the equivalent of the white blood cells in the body's immune system). Trust me, this really happens with people and companies. An idea comes up, people feel threatened by the idea and all of the forces of the status quo unite in order to expel the idea <u>and</u> the person driving it. Sounds lovely, doesn't it? Accept it is a natural reaction. It is far easier to move past this resistance when you understand that there is nothing personal about it. In fact, resistance must occur in order to advance the innovation.

The corporate immune system triggers many of the most common responses to something new and different at companies, such as:

- We've tried that already;
- A program like that already failed;
- This is similar to other programs that have been killed;
- That will never work here;
- Actually, we are doing that! (This is my personal favorite, where people with no better defense claim that they are already doing what you are planning to do.) Typically, upon deeper questioning, the claim is quickly disproven and the person retreats to a defense of "a simple misunderstanding."

There are other factors that support the corporate immune system and prevent innovation from occurring. Past experience can taint the prospects for future success if you use "experience" as a blinder rather than a guide. Good ideas may have been kicked around an organization in the past and failed. This does not mean that it cannot work now or in the future. Some of the more common reasons for innovation failure include:

- Wrong time
- Wrong focus on a feature
- Wrong people on the team
- Wrong target customer
- Unclear value proposition

The corporate immune system is predictable. You know there will be a response. You should expect it, and be prepared to persevere despite the objections raised. Just as is the case with the body's immune system, being exposed to "outside elements" helps make the body stronger over time. If it doesn't kill you, it will make you stronger. Continual exposure to outside matter or innovation will make the corporation stronger, as it does not have the same need to react with a vengeance to repeated exposure. The organization can learn to tolerate innovation exposure over time.

**Lessons learned from *Culture and the Corporate Antibodies That Protect It***

⊙ **There is no culture without you.** Culture does not do anything...people do. The collective experience and learned behavior of all of the individuals in a company define the culture. Culture does not make the people. The people make the culture.

⊙ **Innovation triggers the corporate immune system.** Innovation causes change; change causes resistance and the bigger the change and the faster you move the more resistance you will create. It is a natural reaction, not a sign that innovation cannot be achieved.

⊙ **All change, even good change causes stress.** People resist change to reduce stress.

# 3 | Movement Causes Resistance... The Physics of Innovation

If there is no resistance or corporate antibodies trying to kill you and your idea then you are either not moving fast enough or your idea is not big enough to generate resistance. All change—even good change—triggers resistance. Resistance is a signal that you are doing something that matters. Once you understand this physics equation, it is easy to navigate through the cascade of "no's" that you will hear. In physics, you may recall that Momentum = Velocity x Mass. In order to increase momentum, you either increase the velocity, or the mass. Continuing down this physics refresher course, the greater the momentum, the more resistance you create. In short, moving faster or increasing the mass will in turn increase the resistance on the object being moved.

In corporations, there is a similar rule: Momentum = Speed x Business Impact (Mass). You increase momentum by increasing your speed and/or the size of the business impact (mass). Again, resistance is a natural and predictable reaction to an idea or opportunity (object) being moved in an organization. The faster you move and/or the bigger the business impact, the more resistance you will encounter. It's just the "Physics of Innovation" at work. In short, you need to expect resistance as a natural reaction to something that will create momentum for new business value. It is not a good or bad thing; it is just a law of nature! When you look at it from this perspective it is a lot easier to handle the inevitable obstacles you will face and the resistors behind them.

There is an important "Physics of Innovation" corollary: If you do not encounter resistance to your idea/innovation then it is either not a big enough idea or you are not moving fast enough!

One way to accelerate innovation in an organization is to decrease the resistance. With less resistance, objects in motion will stay in motion longer. Now, given the fine physics refresher course I just reviewed with you, I need to be clear on one critical point: I am not suggesting that you slow down or decrease the business impact in order to minimize resistance. Rather, to eliminate resistance and overcome the corporate antibodies, there are four key strategies:

1. Understand the 5 broad stages of the innovative process
2. Co-create solutions with resistors
3. Classify your efforts as an "experiment"
4. Hear "know" when people say "no."

## Five Stages of the Innovation Process

1. *Insight*— having some customer research/observation that suggests there is a potential opportunity is an important building block for innovation. It helps disarm potential resistors. Customer insight is harder than it appears. Customers have a hard time telling you exactly what innovation would be most meaningful to them. They can, however, leave you clues to piece together to generate the "insight."
2. *Problem Identification*—what is the problem you are going to solve? If the problem you are trying to solve is recognized as business critical, you may have more leeway to try new ways to solve.
3. *Divergent Solutions*—create a diverse list of possible solutions to the problem and work closely with resistors at this stage—make them a part of the solution. It is important to generate a number of alternative solutions to

avoid becoming anchored to the first solution you develop.

4. *Rapid Prototyping/Experimentation*—test the concept quickly and inexpensively to learn what you need to know to be successful.  It is unlikely that you will have it right the first time, so test and adapt (or pivot) based on customer feedback.  If you are accustomed to certainty, you need to get used to disappointment.  There is almost never certainty with any new idea…other than the certainty that you need to learn more with a prototype.  The road to success is paved with failures (or as I prefer to say, learnings).

5. *Lather, Rinse and Repeat*—the experiment generates new customer insight which may sharpen the problem you are trying to solve and lead to new solutions to test.

### Co-Create Solutions with Resistors

The *Divergent Solutions* stage is your opportunity to reach out to those individuals who may be most predisposed to resist your initiative.  Get close to your most likely vocal critics/resistors.  The temptation may be to avoid those who do not support your initiative.  Why subject yourself to the abuse from "non-believers?"  The answer is that you need their insight to help make your initiative better.  Seek those individuals out, enroll them on your team, listen to their concerns/challenges, and let them contribute to the solution early in the solutions development process.  This is how you turn a "would be" enemy into a critical ally or ambassador for the cause.  Embrace the input from potential resistors.  You may find that their creative problem solving skills are pretty darned good even if it is beyond their "functional" expertise.  The benefit of co-creating solutions with resistors is that it creates genuine ownership.  The more that you let people share in the creation of the solution the more ownership they will take in driving the solution to a successful outcome.  They become vested in your success because it feels like their success. This was a critical strategy that enabled the Campus Consumer program [a viral student selling network discussed in Chapter 24] to overcome the corporate antibodies and extend the program into the pharmaceutical side of the business. Everyone had identified "legal" as a potential show-stopping obstacle to the program I was trying to build. I sought out and involved the head legal person and involved her in the development of the solution. With her on board as one of the architects of our approach, we effectively eliminated any potential legal reason to reject the programs expansion. By working closely with resistors, we effectively plowed and sowed the seeds of innovation in the vast fields of corporate sameness! (Not sure what that means, exactly, but after I wrote it, I thought it sounded really cool.)

### Classify Your Efforts as an "Experiment"
We have already discussed the critical role that experiments play in the innovation process. I'd like to dive in a little more into the science behind innovation. Quick audience trivia: Is innovation more of a science or art? Most people would say it is more art than science, but in fact that there is also a lot of "science" involved in innovation. The first science concept we discussed was the physics of resistance and movement. The next important science concept was designing and conducting experiments. If you recall from your own science studies, experiments consist of a hypothesis, a testing methodology (to prove or disprove your hypothesis) and the result of the test. In all cases, there was an outcome of experiments. Whether you prove or disprove your hypothesis, you get exactly what you need: learning. This learning then forms the basis for action if the hypothesis is proven or for subsequent experiments if your hypothesis was not proven with the initial experiment. At no point in science is a failed experiment a failure because it produces the learning from which you can build a successful test. The same is true with experiments that drive innovation.

In the corporate world, there can be too much focus on the black and white of success and failure and not enough focus on the shades of grey in between—this is the "learning." Most projects run their course and either succeed or fail based on the achievement of some critical objective. When you are dealing with innovation and creating new value, it is especially important that the plans are not hard-coded. What I mean, is at the onset of any initiative you rarely know enough of what you need to know to succeed. You need to learn things along the way to success. And the way to do that is with experiments. Each experiment designed to prove/disprove a hypothesis contributes more of the learning you need to achieve success. Importantly, there is no failure in experiments, only learning. You could learn that you are on the right track, or you could learn that there are adjustments that need to be made on the path to success.

There is a very important benefit to learning through experiments as it relates to resistance. By calling initiatives experiments, you are able to keep the corporate antibodies from seeking out and destroying your initiative. Antibodies are seeking out the big projects that threaten the comfort of the status quo in a big way. Experiments are designed to produce learning, not status-quo-threatening change. Classifying your innovation as an experiment keeps the resistance down and the corporate antibodies at bay as it reduces the perceived "mass" or potential business impact (and organizational change) of the initiative. Without the heavy burden of high expectations initially, you have the freedom to make the adjustments necessary to get to a successful outcome. This reclassification of big opportunities into small experiments was critical in order to get the Tailbrands Project [discussed in Chapter 22] and the Campus Consumer Program [discussed in Chapter 24] off the ground. My boss, Ford Calhoun, suggested I call my innovation projects experiments. I admit that I did not like calling my projects experiments as I felt like it made the initiatives sound shoddy and unimportant. But in retrospect, it did allow me to reduce the amount of resistance I got on projects. This allowed me the space I needed to get momentum behind the initiatives. My boss was right. Heck, even with the "experiment" label, the corporate antibodies seemed to be pretty active. I can only imagine how much more aggressively they would have sought my destruction without the experiment disguise!

## Hear "Know" When Others Say "No"

There is an important corollary to the Movement Causes Resistance Theorem: No means "know." Any entrepreneur, innovator or passionate person needs to get comfortable with hearing no. Almost all of the really cool things I created or was involved with over the years had to battle against legions of "no's." I can't control whether someone says no to my idea, but I can determine how I react to hearing "no." I viewed it as a badge of honor when I could force someone into saying "no." The more resistance I would get, the more certain I was onto something big because my idea must really be messing with the keepers of the status quo.

I liken this reinterpretation of "no" to a judo move. When a stronger, heavier opponent (the resistors) attacks, you want to use their momentum coming towards you to re-direct them past you. You would not want to try to stop the attack by meeting force with force. This very simple judo-like move can turn rejection into forward momentum. Every good opportunity I developed started on the same path. I had a vision of something that others did not initially share. I did my best to help them understand the upside opportunity within my vision even as they helped me become aware of my blind spots. Unfortunately, I got the most common (and natural) response regarding nearly every innovation I pursued: "no." Fortunately for me, I am pretty comfortable hearing no from people. In fact, I once attended a theme party in my early days where the objective for the evening was to get people to say "no." Each person at the party started with one bandana and if you said "no" to someone then you had to turn over your bandana to the person who elicited the "no" from you. The combination of my competitive spirit and my ability to attract "no" from people led me to victory that night (and earned me the nickname Bandana Boy). I had little idea that dealing with no could be so helpful in my future innovation pursuits.

So, I performed my "judo" move to turn rejection into positive momentum for my initiative. When people say "no" to me, I hear "know," as in they don't know what I know. I truly believed that if they did know what I knew, then they would support my recommendation. Quite simply, when others say "no" to something new, different, or challenging, you, as an innovator, need to interpret that as "know." What the heck does that mean? Let me tell you... it means that the reason why people say "no" is because they do not "know" enough (yet) to say yes. The important part to this corollary is that the onus of control rests with you rather than your audience. You need to do a better job of communicating the upside benefit of the innovation in order for them to "get it" and say yes. The ball stays in your court when you hear "know." It is up to you to make it meaningful enough (perhaps by increasing the size of the business impact) for them to prioritize your opportunity over the other multitude of priorities competing for the attention of your audience.

"No" just means that you have not convinced them of what you "know." These four principals are what I used to guide me through the labyrinth of approvals necessary to launch the Campus Consumer program which was a selling network of 400 students at 200 universities around the country [detailed in Chapter 24]. I understood the steps in the innovation process. I got very close to my biggest potential resistor—the legal department—and allowed them to help shape the development of our ultimate solution. I started with a small test of the concept—40 students at 20 universities. I overcame the constant barrage of rejection and "no" by listening to the source of the rejection and delivering the information I knew about the program in a way that could be received by those who were saying "no."

⊙ ⊙ ⊙

## Lessons learned from *Movement Causes Resistance... The Physics of Innovation*

⊙ **Innovation requires change and change attracts resistance.** Even good change causes stress so people naturally resist it. The tension caused by this resistance can lead to even better outcomes as you overcome the obstacles standing in the way of your success.

⊙ **Resistance is a sign that you are onto something!** If there is no resistance, your idea is not big enough or you are not moving fast enough. The bigger the impact and the faster you move, the greater the resistance you will create. That's how you know you are on to something.

⊙ **You can minimize resistance by:**

O Understanding the steps in the innovation process: insight, problem identification, divergent solutions, rapid prototyping/experimentation, "lather, rinse, and repeat."

O Co-creating your solution with resistors. Get close to those people who are most likely to resist the change driven by your innovation and make them part of the solution.

O Classifying your efforts as an "experiment." Experiments attract less resistance than the typical far-reaching corporate project that impacts many people across the organization.  Stay low.

O Hear "know" when people say "no."  You will face rejection throughout the innovation journey.  It is important that you help people "know" what you know in order to overcome their resistance.

# 4 | "Stand-up" for What You Believe

This story highlights the importance of standing up for what you believe in. Obstacles will often arise and you need to use your passion to overcome obstacles that others may put in your way. Ironically, the very inclusion of this story in my book is another telling example of the relentless pursuit of your beliefs. I had some feedback from well-meaning reviewers that this story is not about innovation. I accept that feedback on some level but believe it is very important to understand the "mindset" of an innovator when faced with opposition. Feel free to give me feedback on my stance: **feedback@diaryofaninnovator.com**.

I had the great fortune of having a powerfully important learning experience during my senior year in high school. The learning I am talking about had nothing to do with academics. I was a pretty good student and enjoyed academic learning, mind you, but all of that learning paled in comparison to the life-long lesson from for my Senior Variety Show at my high school, Conestoga in Berwyn, PA.

In the variety show, I had planned to be in a group comedic sketch with a number of my friends and classmates. The sketch was a mock of the *Newlywed Game*—with a bunch of bizzaro characters as the married guests—from the prim and proper Biff and Muffy to the aliens from *Saturday Night Live* fame, the Coneheads. I played the role of Beldar Conehead. Since it was a group comedy sketch, it was easy to play off of one another and bring out the best in each other. During all of our rehearsals, we would systematically convert spontaneous changes from the rehearsal into the plan for the show. It was a really cool, iterative process (an early lesson in rapid prototyping!). That sketch turned out to be a lot of fun...and was pretty darned funny based on the audience reaction.

I also planned to do a solo stand-up comedy routine. I would be out there on my own. It was a little daunting if I stopped to think about it. Fortunately, I never stopped to think about it. I always thought that I had a pretty good sense of humor, as far as I knew anyway, and definitely was not afraid to laugh at my own jokes. After all, sometimes people need permission to believe you are funny. My laughter was their permission. My friends use to make comments, "You think you are so funny." I did...and thanks for the observation.

I was pretty excited about the prospect of doing my own thing and really looked forward to coming up with some material—some of which would be "borrowed" and some of which was my own. I shared this excitement for my act with my friends and family and was counting on them to be a supportive force in this endeavor.

Much to my surprise, there was almost universal concern and negativity expressed by friends and family. Rather than encourage and support me, everyone was trying to talk me out of doing it. I could not believe it. Why were they all so against me trying to do something that clearly was a passion of mine? Did they truly not care enough to support me in this project? Or was it something deeper?

It was a little troubling, but I did not let it stop me. While their support certainly would have been nice, I remained very determined. And the more that people voiced opposition to my plan, the deeper my resolve for success became. "I'll show them!" You may think I'm just writing that for effect, but it is truly how I felt. I really wanted to show everyone who doubted me just how damn funny I could be. There was a direct correlation between the amount of opposition I faced and the determination I had to succeed. The greater the concern expressed, the greater the determination to succeed (damn them all!). [In a nod to those who advised me of the irrelevance of this chapter, innovators and entrepreneurs thrive on proving doubters wrong!]

It was during the course of one of my discussions with a friend that I started to realize the root of everyone's opposition. One friend asked me a very simple question: "What if you are not funny?" Huh, I never really thought of that. It had never really occurred to me that I would not be funny. I'm hilarious. How could I ever not be funny? I'm funny by accident most times. I just blurt out something before my brain can intervene and stop my comment from seeing the light of day. Without even thinking about my response, I replied confidently, "I will be funny." In my mind, there was no option but to be funny, so it was inconceivable to me that I would "not" be funny. To me, failure was not an option.

What I failed to appreciate fully until much, much later in life was that my friends and family were objecting to my stand-up comedy routine out of love and concern rather than disinterest or malice. They were genuinely concerned about how I might react to a situation where I performed my routine and was simply not funny. Or, if they wanted to put it more gently to me: "What if the audience does not 'get' your humor?" Would I be able to handle that? So, while the motive for the lack of universal support from friends and family was truly noble, it still had no sway on me. In fact, it gave me even more motivation to succeed. I love a challenge—particularly one that others believe to be impossible. It's more fun to win when everyone believes you will lose. It's also more fun to win, when everyone else is afraid to even compete!

Despite the vociferous objections of those close to me, I proceeded with my plans. I practiced the routine day after day leading up to the show. It was only through this repetition that I had my first real concern myself. After I did the jokes over and over again, they sort of lost their luster with me. They were funny the first dozen times, sure, but the last couple of dozen times, the stories just sounded old because I had heard them before. It was a challenge to deliver the routine with a consistently high level of energy day after day.

The other issue I was facing is that my rehearsals did not have a huge audience and those who were there had also heard the material over and over again. It was the same group of people—all of whom were performing in the show. To me it was like seeing the old M*A*S*H TV shows. Every now and then, they would do a show with no audience laugh track. The same writers, the same actors and the material just did not seem to be as funny because there were no signals from others that it was funny. There was no "permission to believe." That was a little bit of what I was experiencing. I had to remind myself that the success metric for my routine would not be how funny it was to me, rather how funny it was to the audience, who would be hearing the material for the first time. I convinced myself that I was going to have the opportunity to introduce my material to a fresh audience on two consecutive nights, and that I would feed off of their fresh reaction to my "stuff."

When the weekend of the shows finally arrived, I was pretty excited. I will now admit something that most performers are afraid to admit. I was a little bit nervous before the show. I was about to perform my routine on two consecutive nights in front of nearly 1000 people each night! A little scary, I will confess, but man was it fun! I will never forget the incredible adrenaline rush I had just before the curtain opened for my act. It was one of the most amazing feelings I have ever experienced. The curtain parted and out I walked on stage. With stage lights glaring in my eyes I could not actually see the entire audience, but I knew they were there. All I was thinking about was performing the show and absolutely "killing it!" I was going to be really funny. I just knew it.

I warmed up the audience with a quick teaser. I informed them that I was going to start my segment with a near impossible feat. I was going to juggle three tennis balls while jumping rope at the same time. As intended, this brought the audience in. I had a canister of 3 tennis balls in one hand and a jump rope in the other. I carefully took the three tennis balls out of the canister, and started with a quick warm-up juggle. I then carefully laid out the jump rope on the stage and looked knowingly into the audience. I stepped back behind the rope I had just laid across the stage and started juggling the tennis balls. Then I announced that I was now going to begin jumping rope while juggling. I then jumped over the rope and kept on juggling. The crowd went wild. And then I announced that I was now going to jump rope backwards, and proceeded to jump back over the rope on the stage. Again, the crowd loved it. The rest of my routine—stories and jokes—went even better than I had hoped. The audience roared with laughter. I can't even begin to tell you what an incredible rush that was…but then again, maybe I just did. It was amazing!

You may be wondering what this story has to do with innovation. To me, the lessons are clear. This experience was the beginning of my journey down the road of innovation. I had overcome the overt resistance of well-meaning friends and family to accomplish something that was a passion of mine. Passion is what enabled me to overcome the obstacles that others placed in my path. And, it is really important to have the power of belief on your side. I had total confidence in my ability to get things done and I got it done. I never let the doubt of others seep into my mind and erode my confidence and desire to accomplish my goal.  In fact, the doubt of others fueled my desire to succeed.  This was also the first time that I heard "know" when others said "no."  Clearly they did not know that I was going to be funny, and that's why they said no. I was confident I would be…and that's what I knew!

⊙ ⊙ ⊙

## Lessons learned for *"Stand-up"* for What You Believe

⊙ **I am damn funny!**  Even if I'm the only one that believes it, that's alright with me.  The real lesson is to follow your passion.

⊙ **Follow your passion.**  I wanted to do stand-up comedy and nobody could talk me out of it.

⊙ **Resistance is a constant.**  You must accept it is as a natural part of the journey towards success.

⊙ **The power of belief is stronger than the power of doubt.** Do not let the doubt expressed by others weaken your resolve. Instead, use it as a catalyst for overcoming obstacles.

⊙ **If you think you can, you can.**  Believe in yourself.  You truly can do anything you think you can.  Too often, we fall victim to the belief that things are too difficult or impossible before we even try.  Try…and then find the path to success.

# 5 | The Power of Networking... Bowling for Contacts!

This story is a lesson on the importance of networking—especially early in your career. You never know who knows whom. I really had no idea what I was doing in my first job out of undergraduate, but the way I secured that job was a huge lesson in the power of networking. Not only did networking help me get my first full-time job out of college, but it also helped me establish a core group of friends/colleagues (aka, my "network") who have been incredibly valuable to me both personally and professionally for decades.

This networking story began in the second semester of my senior year at Duke. I was living the good life. My good life was actually quite annoying to many of my friends. I think it had something to do with my "demanding" schedule as a part-time student. I had two classes—one of which met at 3:00pm on Mondays and the other met at 3:45pm on Tuesdays. That was it. No classes the rest of the week. I tried to sell the "part-time" student concept to my parents by explaining that part-time status would allow me to concentrate on finding a job after graduation. After all, job interviews would take a lot of time from my studies. Dad was not sold on this concept at all. He was not buying it. He wanted me to be a full-time student. I then tailored my message a little by focusing on something he was actually "buying"—my tuition. I indicated that as a "part-time" student, I ("we" would be far more accurate in this case since he paid tuition) only had to pay for the classes I attend. Fewer classes meant lower tuition. He was suddenly pretty enthusiastic about this cost-effective approach to my studies.

As it turned out, I did actually have a lot of interviews all over the country, so I was not totally disingenuous to my original story line. Ideally, I wanted to find a job opportunity in the Philadelphia area where I grew up. There were not many opportunities there. My roommate, Joe Payne, actually stumbled across one of them during one of his many interviews. After his interview with the SmithKline Beckman recruiter, he suggested that I wangle my way into an interview with them. It was a pharmaceutical company based in Philadelphia and offered new hires a Management Associate training program. The program allowed you to rotate through different functions (e.g. marketing, sales, finance, manufacturing, etc.) in different divisions of the organization over a two-year period. That sounded perfect for me as I had no idea what role I would ultimately aspire to. This would give me the opportunity to figure it out "on the job."

I attempted, to no avail, to squirm into an interview that day while the recruiter was on-campus to no avail. I then sent a letter to the recruiter back in Philadelphia expressing my strong interest in the position and requesting an interview. Finally, and most importantly, I sent a letter to Mr. Byrnes, who was the father of a boy with whom I played Little League baseball when I was 8-years-old. Mr. Byrnes happened to be the President of SmithKline Chemicals—one of the major divisions of the company. I thought that he might be able to help get my resume to the right people at SmithKline Beckman.

I heard two replies from the recruiter at SmithKline Beckman. The first one was a generic "thanks but no thanks" letter saying that they will keep my resume on file in case a "suitable" opportunity arises. Everyone knows when they receive this type of letter that the only "file" they have is the trash file. The second letter arrived a few days later and said that they would be happy to interview me for a Management Associate (MA) position if I was able to get to Philadelphia. Hmmm, this seemed to me at the time to be a strange set of circumstances. They first rejected my interest and then within the same week, they embraced it. What could have changed their mind? Well, as it turns out, the letter I sent Mr. Byrnes led to him contacting HR with a suggestion that they interview me.

I went to Philadelphia for the interview, did really well and was offered a job with SmithKline Beckman. That was my first real exposure to the power of networking. I did not have any intention when I was 8 years old of developing relationships that would later prove valuable to me, but I did learn that everyone matters in this world and that you should treat others the way that you would want to be treated. Mr. Byrnes helped open my first door into the business world 14 years later.

You may be wondering what the first thing I did when I was offered the job. Well, first, I enthusiastically accepted the position and quickly followed with a question of my own. I tried to figure out the latest possible date that I could start. I was told that there was two start dates for incoming MAs—one in June and the other in September. That's all I needed to hear. "Sign me up for September! Have a nice summer." I needed a break, after all, to recover from my grueling senior schedule (remember, I had two classes in the last semester!). I had a great summer and I came up with a terrific plan for late summer and early fall. Since my girlfriend at the time was a rising senior, I thought I would just join her back at Duke for the first 3 weeks of the school year. I was back at Duke—the gothic wonderland! Many people who knew (or at least thought they knew) that I had graduated were a bit confused by my presence. Just to have a little fun, I would let on that I had failed to take enough credits and simply needed a ½ credit physical education course to graduate. It was surprising how many people bought that story.

All good things must come to an end, and alas, I eventually left

Duke and started my job at SmithKline Beckman. I met a lot of very interesting people in my "class" of 13 management associates. I quickly sized them up and put everyone into two buckets—the group of people I would go out and have beers with and the rest. To this day, twenty-six years later, I still stay in fairly regular contact with 6 or 7 of those people, and yes, I have had many, many beers with them over the years. How did this strong bond get established?

I have always been a pretty gregarious, social person and I carried these characteristics and personal tendencies into my first job. The job itself was pretty interesting but not nearly as interesting as the things my job enabled me to do...now that I was making real money. There were a number of fellow MAs who I thought would be fun to hang with in a social setting. Rather than wait for something to spontaneously occur, I decided to organize an event that would bring all (or at least most) of us together in a fun and relaxed environment.

Again, like my experience with Mr. Brynes, there was no grand plan or thoughtful plot to develop this "social network." In fact, "social networking" had not even been invented yet! I was young, gregarious and enjoyed having fun on the weekends. I thought it would be great if we could get all of the Management Associates together each month for a few rounds of bowling (and beer). It would be an opportunity for us to catch up on work stuff—since we were dispersed across many different parts of the business. And, more importantly, it would allow me to test the assumption I made from day one about which people belonged in which bucket. As it turned out, I was right about the folks that I thought I'd enjoy a beer with.

I also had my first corporate experience with "experiments" at these "Bowlarama" events. I conducted an experiment designed to determine the impact of beer intake on the bowling scores of the management associates. I was able to generate fascinating learning while having a lot of fun during the testing phase! The results were semi-intuitive. Beer did have an impact on bowling scores. Apparently, scores get better after one or two beers, gets worse with three to four, and improves again with five or six. After six beers, the scores dropped precipitously. I actually created a graphical representation of this phenomenon that I called the "Anheuser Curve," in honor of our Bowlarama beer of choice.

These monthly events went on for a year or two and when the next class of MAs joined the company, many of them were invited to participate as well. It really was a pretty cool social network...long before networks were enabled by the internet or mobile communications.

One of the other things that the Bowlarama experience taught me was that there are always ripple effects from action. There was one MA who complained to our HR Manager that I had excluded him from the Bowlarama events. Truth be told, I had no idea who he was since our paths never crossed, and it was just chance that we did not have a broader invite list for these events. Keep in mind...we did not have e-mail or texting of any sort at this time. It really was a case of people you knew, or at least knew their phone number, and then you'd call them directly and invite them.

Despite all of these seemingly rational explanations for the inadvertent exclusion of this individual, my boss at the time suggested to me that I had created an exclusive group of MAs and that some people felt like they were on the outside looking in. I was flabbergasted. Nobody had asked me to set up a social event in the first place. I was not doing it for the benefit of the company. I was doing it because I thought it would be a lot of fun to socialize with other like-minded, younger employees in a predominantly older organization. I felt like I was being criticized for demonstrating a little initiative. This was my first important lesson in innovation within companies. The Bowlarama events were not technically an innovation, but it was something new that MAs had never done before, and with anything new, there will be resistors and detractors. I just never expected one of the MAs to be a critic—especially since he had not been singled out in any way. He had just not been in the same circles. How do you deal with resistors or detractors? Get closer to them to understand what makes them tick. And that's what I did. I called the disgruntled MA to ask if he'd like to join the next Bowlarama.

It did not take long for him to feel like a part of the team. As it turns out, he was actually a pretty interesting guy with a good sense of humor and added quite a bit to the future Bowlarama events. I definitely became more conscious of thinking through potential ripple effects of my actions thereafter—which was a good learning early in my career as I had no idea just how naïve I was. I was too naïve to recognize my own naivety.

◉ ◉ ◉

## Lessons learned from *The Power of Networking... Bowling for Contacts!*

◉ **Build your network early.** Treat everyone you meet the way you would want to be treated. This is how you build a strong network that can be a valuable asset for you to leverage down the road.

◉ **Leverage your network.** Having a network is important, but the value is unlocked when you leverage your network. You never know who people know. Ask. Don't be afraid to ask people you know for a favor for things important to you.

⊙ **Anything "new" causes stress.** Even a fun social event created stress among fellow management associates who felt like they were on the outside looking in.

⊙ **Resistance to "new" is inevitable.** It is natural and should not stop you from pursuing your initiative. Anticipate it and seek to minimize or mitigate it by getting closer to the biggest detractors.

⊙ **There are always unintended consequences.** When you learn of them, they should become "new information," not bad news.

# 6 | "Self-Selection" Tips the Scales of Success

This story is about unleashing the power of self-selection on experiments. Allowing people to "self-select" into opportunities or experiments based on their passions increases the likelihood of achieving success—which is particularly important for innovators. Wharton was undertaking a huge task of revamping their already successful business school curriculum just as I was matriculating into the MBA graduate program. They accomplished this task by conducting a curriculum "experiment" with two cohorts of students to better understand that which they did not know. Interestingly, many of the students who played a critical role in the evolution and success of the new curriculum had self-selected into the new curriculum. They wanted to be a part of the experiment. They welcomed the opportunity to explore a new and different curriculum and appreciated the opportunity to shape it. Their passion for their role helped accelerate the learning necessary to evolve the curriculum. This story begins with my departure from SmithKline Beckman.

After 4 years of working at SmithKline Beckman (which later became SmithKline Beecham), I decided that it was time for me to broaden my horizons and pursue my MBA at the University of Pennsylvania's Wharton School of Business. I wanted to have the opportunity to learn from the best that business school had to offer to prepare me for starting and running my own business. Heck, I had already received an outstanding business education from my various rotational assignments as a Management Associate (HR, Sales, Marketing and National

Accounts Marketing), but I wanted more. An MBA from Wharton would give me the sort of credentials necessary to attract the sort of management talent and investors I would need to start my own business.

I learned a valuable lesson about working hard to do your best in everything you do. Having done well on prior standardized tests, I assumed I would do well on the GMATs, a standardized test of math, English, critical reasoning required by most business schools. I did not prepare adequately and did not do as well on the test as I would have liked. I was denied admission in my first attempt in part because my GMAT scores were not stellar—a mediocre 590. In short, I had not studied enough to prepare myself for the rigors of the test. I thought I could rely on my "baseline" smarts to get a top score on the test. Apparently my baseline smarts needed a little "honing." The next go-around, I would take no chances. I signed up for a Stanley Kaplan course that helped me prepare and gave me tips for taking the test to help eliminate the chance of a wrong answer. The result was impressive. My score increased 120 points to 710. So, with another year of great work experience under my belt and a GMAT score in the top 5%, I was accepted at Wharton. There is a two-fold lesson here. First, don't take anything for granted. Second, if you really want something, you need to give it your all. Go after it as if your life depended on it. I really wanted to go to Wharton and I had to do everything I could to get the best score on the GMAT.

Just a few months before school was to begin in September, my brother, Larry, sent me an article in *BusinessWeek* about a new curriculum that was being launched at Wharton. This new curriculum would transform the business school experience and better prepare graduates for the increasing demands for global perspective, cross-functional expertise, and collaboration in teams. The courses themselves would be "team taught" across functions—we would follow the same case study from different functional perspectives across our marketing, operations and finance classes. Additionally, the new curriculum started one month earlier in order to create time for the "softer" side teaching, e.g. organizational management and psychology. Finally, there was another very cool requirement that all students would participate in a 5-6 week business "immersion" tour to either Germany or Japan.

This sounded awesome. Totally new! Totally cool! I wanted in on this opportunity. Now the only problem was that the article indicated that the participants in the 2 experimental cohorts (there were also 11 traditional cohorts) were to be selected "randomly." I always thought of myself as a "random" guy, so I felt my chances were good. That said, I did my best to become part of the random sample by sending a letter to the Dean of Admissions requesting that I be permitted to participate in one of the two experimental cohorts. As "luck" would have it, I was then "randomly" selected.

When I got to school in August—a full month before the "traditional" program participants arrived—I met a bunch of other hard charging, but fun-loving individuals who had done some amazing things in their prior business experience. And I was pleasantly surprised at the entrepreneurial/self-starter vibe that most folks had. As it turned out, nearly every student leadership position at Wharton would eventually be occupied by a member of the two "pilot" cohorts, including the entire student government cabinet, the student newspaper, and most of the other significant organizations. I thought it was very interesting and it made me even more curious about the "random" selection of pilot program participants.

One of the other things I learned as I talked to more of my fellow classmates—both traditional and non-traditional—was that the selection "randomness" was not as random as you would expect. I met a number of people in the traditional program who were asked to participate but who declined because they wanted the "known" curriculum that was ranked top 3 in the country at the time. Their thinking was: Why settle for the uncertain and unknown when you can have the best of what is known? I saw things differently. I was still attracted by the appeal of the shiny new penny the school was holding up versus the crusty, old, decaying one that represented what "was" at Wharton. So I asked for it…and got it. Even more interesting, I found a remarkable number of people who were also "randomly" selected for the new curriculum after they called or sent a letter (this is before e-mail existed!) requesting that they be a part of it. In other words, the right people found their way to the program—they self-selected in! I am convinced that this self-selection bias helped ensure the program's success. We all knew it would be a bumpy ride but we were up for the challenge.

Me, personally, I always prefer the new and different to the old way. This new program was perfect for me. I feel a John Candy reference coming on from *Stripes* after he enlisted in the Army (not a direct quote, just all that I could remember): "And you got…what…a six to eight week training program here? A real tough one? Which is perfect for me. I'm gonna walk out of here a lean, mean, fighting machine." At Wharton they changed the traditional 13-week semester courses to 6-week mini-modules…which is perfect for those of us who are "attention challenged" and those of us who wanted to walk out a lean, mean, business machine. There was no time to lose focus in 6 weeks. I did ask one of the accounting professors what the difference was between the traditional 13-week and new 6-week courses he taught. I expected to hear a very thoughtful reply that reflected the careful consideration that Wharton must have gone through prior to approving the plan to evolve their curriculum. I expected words like, "highly integrated," and "more collaborative;" these were the words used to describe the new curriculum to the prospective students and the rest of the outside world. I did not expect to hear the actual words he said, which were: Well, we basically cover the same amount of material with fewer examples. Great! That's what I'm looking for! A full semester course crammed into 6 weeks....and we get to take twice as many classes. I guess that means I earned a 4-year MBA degree (hey, that's unique!) in just 2 years! Who else can say that? My glass is half-full.

A funny thing happened as I began to experience Wharton's innovative new curriculum, though. Things did not appear to be as "fully-baked" as they were purported to be. In fact, I'm not even sure that the ingredients had been purchased for the batter, as was not clear that the faculty, (the bakers), were involved in co-creating the future curriculum (more on this later). Although we were very clearly identified as the "pilot" cohorts, I was still expecting that some of the things we were going through would have been a bit smoother. The morning Tai Chi classes on the quad—which sounded so revolutionary for a business school—quickly disappeared. The class workload for these highly integrated cross-functional classes was incredibly demanding and not altogether integrated as it had been advertised. There seemed to be a fairly major disconnect between the vision that was communicated from the administration to the incoming class of students and what became the practice in the classroom.

This experience highlighted the importance of getting close to those who are most likely to be resistant to change. In this case, the tenured faculty in well-established departmental silos were responsible for delivering the curriculum. They were absolutely resistant to the changes that the new experimental cohorts necessitated. I can tell you from my own teaching experience at Wharton and Villanova that it takes a lot of work to develop the materials for a new course. Once you have the course material down, you can really focus on fine tuning the content and delivering the material with more impact. What the administration failed to anticipate is that there would be massive faculty resistance to the new curriculum that was being proposed. It would involve an enormous amount of time for each teacher to make the changes to a course that was already running smoothly. The administration should have gotten closer to the faculty in order to let them co-create the new program and have them take a greater ownership stake in the rollout of those changes.

From the student side of things, this failure of the administration and the faculty to work constructively to co-create the new curriculum had a big impact on what we felt. I had never experienced anything like this. There was so much work, it was literally impossible to get it all done. I rationalized that this must have been a part of their plan from the start. They must be trying to teach us that if there is too much work for anyone to do it all you MUST rely on your team to get everything done. We certainly felt the pain of the lack of communication between the administration and the staff. We saw early signs of it when the students gave feedback that the workload was completely out-of-control. That's when we learned that the "overload leading to better team collaboration" was not by design.

The cause of the overload was the administration's failure to communicate to professors the same message that they were communicating to the students and the rest of the world. Professors who were running pilot classes did not re-work their class work and integrate it with other classes as the administration had promised to students. Instead, professors jammed 13 full weeks of course material into 6 weeks—and took out a lot of the examples that they would have otherwise used to help explain key points. The overload we felt was an unintended consequence of really bad communication and a failure of the interested parties to work together to co-create a solution that worked for the students, faculty and administration. It was not a thoughtful learning objective. The optimist in me would call that a "collateral benefit" as I do believe participants in the pilot program benefited from having the challenge to manage an incredibly burdensome overload.

We were the pilot group... the test. And true to form for all things involving innovation, the only thing you know for sure is that whatever you thought the solution should look like (in this case, the new curriculum), you are wrong. You just don't know how wrong and in what direction. There were lots of ways Wharton was wrong with this pilot program, but that is why they started with a pilot—to find out what works and what needs to change. When they launched the pilot they simply did not know where things were wrong and how they should adapt to get closer to "right." To Wharton's immense credit, they launched a pilot that had dozens of "i's" not dotted and "t's" not crossed. They could have spent years researching the right formula for a new curriculum, and even then it would not have been perfect. Instead, they put their best thinking into an initial pilot that they launched, learned quickly from and adapted. This was even more incredible considering how much emphasis the school put on research.

Another major "snafu" surfaced in the second semester as the students prepared for the German or Japanese immersion tour—which was designed to give students broad exposure to the top leadership at various businesses and industries in these countries. This was really the crown jewel of the new program, and students viewed this as the "pay-off" for the pain and suffering associated with being a part of the experimental group. The immersion tour had been described as a part of the new curriculum—not as an option. Therefore, all of the students believed that the cost of the trip was covered by the school as a part of their tuition payment. This sounded like a deal that was too good to be true.

It was. The administration at Wharton asked each of the pilot program participants to pony up another $6K for the trip, which for students—who are not making any money—was an unanticipated shock to the system. There was a wholesale mutiny among the pilot program students. Again, one of those "collateral benefits" of being part of something new, and only partially baked. Those poor "traditional" students never had the opportunity to meet as a group (115 showed for the "We're Not Going to Take It" meeting") where some of the more articulate folks suggested we have a strong case and that we need to hold our ground until the school agrees that we were misled and that the school should pay for the additional costs we were being asked to pay. Some of the less articulate—emboldened by the beer consumed at the Wharton Pub just prior to our meeting—may have used language that was a bit more "colorful." One of my buddies in fact, who otherwise was a very mild-mannered and reserved person had an alcohol-induced rant that highlighted a number of egregious violations that the school had made, and followed each statement with: "and that's messed up!" He used a different word for "messed." After the 10th or 11th refrain, I think the mob realized that they had seen this movie before and wanted to move on to the next "scene." He got the hint and ceded the floor. For my part, I was pleased to reflect on the fact that our little sociological experience yielded good results—the masses agreed to go forward with one voice to the administration to make the case for no additional costs to the already over-burdened students.

At the end of the day, Wharton got the Ombudsman involved to settle this dispute. I must say that until this experience, I had no idea that there was such a person, but I was thankful there was. The Ombudsman listened carefully to a representative sample of students and administrators and came up with a solution that she felt was fair given the circumstances. The ruling came in as follows: students would have to pay $1000 to help defer some of the costs that the school would incur in order to run the immersion tour. This was a pretty good deal considering that airfare alone would cost almost that much. Neither side got exactly what they wanted, but it was a fair resolution. Nice work by the Ombudsman!

Many of these curriculum growing pains were identified and solutions suggested at the Review and Assessment committee meetings. The Review and Assessment committee was charged with tracking and reporting on the progress of the experimental cohorts. It consisted of key administrators, faculty from the current curriculum, corporate sponsors (like the CEO of P&G and Managing Director of McKinsey) and two student representatives of which I was one. As is often the case, communication to the key parties involved was a big issue for the administration. It was clear that the administration had a vision of the changes that they wanted to make to the curriculum. They did a good job of gaining the support of some of the critical external corporate sponsors, e.g. P&G, McKinsey, etc. After all, the sponsors had a vested interest in the success of the new curriculum as they "consumed" the students that Wharton produced. The administration also did a good job of "attracting enough students to participate in the two pilot cohorts. Where communications broke down, however, was with the faculty charged with teaching the new courses. The administration failed to give them the critical details of the new vision—which resulted in a big disconnect between what the students were promised and what the faculty ultimately delivered. We would meet as a group periodically throughout the year to address the problems as they arose.

One particular Review and Assessment meeting stood out in my mind. I had arrived for the lunch meeting from one of my classes and ambled up to the conference room table just as the meeting was about to begin. Most of the seats had already been taken. There was a seat open next to an elderly gentleman so I staked my claim, and introduced myself and chatted with him before the meeting began (I had no idea who he was or why he was there, by the way). He turned out to be a very nice, articulate gentleman, who introduced himself to me as Peter and seemed to know an awful lot about the change-management challenges we were facing as we transitioned the curriculum from the old to the new. I still could not figure out what he was doing at this meeting, so I finally asked him. He humbly communicated to me that he had been asked to talk a bit about change management, as it was something that Wharton needed to understand given the massive undertaking regarding the curriculum change. That sounded good to me. I was really curious to hear what he had to say.

His presentation—most of it extemporaneous—was riveting. He was awesome. It was like he had a window into our changing world. He gave a 20-minute presentation to the committee. After his presentation, I gave him a hearty congratulation on a job well done. I told him that I thought his presentation was outstanding and really helpful given the challenges that Wharton was facing. He said quite humbly and in accent that I could not quite place, "Thank you, Tom. It is very kind of you to say that." This was a heavy hitting group— except for me and the other student rep, of course. And while the gentleman clearly knew his stuff and his presentation was spot on, I still could not figure out what his role was with the team.

We finished the lunch meeting and I bade farewell to my new friend, Peter. Later that afternoon, one of my friends asked me if I was going to attend a presentation from one of the greatest business management luminaries of all time.... someone who had written more books on marketing, management and other business-related topics than almost anyone. I told my friend that I was not sure, but I wanted to know who this amazing speaker was. He told me the speaker was Peter Drucker. If he had hit me with a 2x4 I'm not sure I would have been more stunned. Whoa! Wait a minute. Was it possible that this luminary "Peter Drucker" was the same Peter that I sat next to at lunch? Say it wasn't so. Uh, yea, Einstein…that's the guy! Boy, did I feel like a dope. I must have been the only one at our committee meeting that had no clue who this guy was. He was just a really smart, interesting, articulate insightful older guy as far as I knew. Now it made sense why Peter was at the meeting presenting to the committee on change management. I was clueless. In retrospect, I'm guessing that Peter may have appreciated the fact that I did not fawn all over him as many students would if they had recognized him for who he was. I was certainly not the sharpest tool in the tool shed to say the least.

To Wharton's immense credit, they proceeded with the transition to the new curriculum and used the learning from the first "pilot" year to set the stage for a more substantial pilot in year 2. Finally, in the third year, having the benefit of two years of making mistakes (and learning), the "new" curriculum became the "only" curriculum. The transition was complete. Although it was at times quite painful to be a part of the experiment, it did give me a great perspective on the challenges that organizations face when they drive change. It is never easy. Be prepared to learn along the way to success.

The implications for a company that wants to evolve to a more innovative culture are huge. You have to articulate clearly the "culture" you seek, and allow the right people to self-select into the evolving organization. You can't expect that you already have the right people in the right spots operating the right way. Set the vision, communicate it widely, and let the right people self-select into your company based on what your company does. The right people will find their way.

◉ ◉ ◉

## Lessons learned from *"Self-Selection" Tips the Scales of Success*

◉ **Allow passionate people to self-select into opportunities.**
Successful innovation and change is more likely when you let
people self-select into the opportunities of greatest interest to
them. The pilot program succeeded because the participants
self-selected into the program and wanted to be part of the
imperfect experiment. Many people were excited about the
prospect of shaping the future of the Wharton experience and
that motivated them to self-select into the program.

◉ **Experiments lead to better and faster results than
research.** Wharton could have spent years researching their
way to a new curriculum and even then it would not have been
perfect. Instead, they put their best thinking into the design of
an initial pilot, launched and learned quickly. Within 3 years,
the transformation of the curriculum was complete.

◉ **Don't wait for "perfect."** Experiments are not perfect—and
don't expect them to be. If Wharton had waited for all of the
stars to align (e.g. faculty to be fully on-board and supportive)
then there would have never been a new curriculum.

◉ **Change—even good change—is difficult and triggers
resistance from those who nurture the status quo**. Change
makes people uncomfortable and causes people to resist. It is
natural and does not signal that the change is bad…just a
change.

⊙ **Focus on the end game of success, not the tactics for getting there.** Wharton wanted to evolve their curriculum to be more cross-functional and integrated. They did not know everything they had to do to achieve their goal. They had to get started and learn along the way. They did not hold any of their initial tactics sacred and that allowed them to adapt as they learned more about what it takes to succeed with the new curriculum.

⊙ **Be yourself around everyone.** I had no idea that I was sitting next to the legendary business guru, Peter Drucker. I engaged him as I would any person, not as the superstar that he was. I think he appreciated our very genuine interaction.

# 7 | Persistence Pays—
## A Passport: Don't Leave
## Home Without It!

This story is about the inner-qualities that allow innovators to succeed in the face of formidable obstacles. While it is not an innovation per se, it is a heck of a good story (as far as I know), so I'm going with it. At the end of the day, innovation requires individuals to overcome a lot! This story details an adventure I had getting into and out of Austria without a passport. What is the tie-in to innovation, you might ask? Well, it comes down to persistence, perseverance, and not knowing (or believing) that something is impossible. Where there is a will, there is a way. Sometimes, not having good options is all the motivation you need to succeed. So, here is the story.

As discussed in Chapter 6, the overhaul of the curriculum at Wharton, was driven by two "experimental" cohorts that had (among other things) a much greater emphasis on international business. At the end of the first year, students had the opportunity to go to either Japan or Germany for a month long immersion into the culture and business of those respective countries. For me, the decision was simple. Beer… springtime… Germany… what's not to like about that? Oh, and did I mention that my best friend from my high school days, Steve Luttmann, was working for Unilever in Vienna, Austria. And get this…I was able to communicate with my buddy in Vienna from Philadelphia for free, on this really cool thing called the "internet." In 1992, that was a pretty cool innovation! Anyway, Luttmann and I agreed that during the trip, I would find a weekend to meet up with him in Vienna to check out the scene.

After significant preparation from the school about the "do's" and "don'ts" associated with our immersion into the German culture, we finally began the journey. The first leg of our German road trip got off to a great start. I flew with a bunch of other Wharton knuckleheads to Frankfurt, Germany on a very entertaining overnight flight. I had planned to catch some shut-eye on the flight, but my buddies had other ideas. The plane ran out of alcoholic drinks and I dare say that the group I was with was probably responsible for that little problem. We were young, and apparently, very, very thirsty. But I digress. We arrived in Frankfurt and took up residence in the Bundespost—which was the training facility for German postal workers. This was our base camp for the German immersion tour. We affectionately referred to it as the "postal prison."

Among the more interesting road trips a few of my buddies and I made was to Prague, Czechoslovakia (before they split into two countries). The key lesson from this story—perhaps the subject of another book—is the power of "win-win." When we crossed the border into Czechoslovakia, the car and passengers were both dangerously low on "fuel;" we needed to fill up with gas, and replenish our stock of liquid refreshments. As luck would have it, the gas station had a case of Pilsner Urquell which would satisfy the very thirsty passengers on the trip. We were elated to find that the case of beer cost the equivalent of $12 or roughly $0.50/beer. This was a huge discount versus what we had experienced in Germany. We were literally high-fiving each other in the car thinking that we just got a great bargain and that this good luck was a harbinger of a tremendous weekend in front of us.

As it turned out, I believe that the attendants at the gas station had a similar feeling of elation over their great fortune to sell us the beer for the price we paid. Once we got to Prague, we realized that the "market price" for the beer we had bought was closer to $0.10/beer. I'm sure the attendants were high-fiving each other as soon as we left. That was a classic win-win. We were happy to pay less than what we had been paying in Germany, and the attendants were happy that they got 5x what they would normally get if they had sold it to Czechoslovakians. It was all good!

My other big road trip was the aforementioned trip from Munich, Germany to visit my friend in Vienna, Austria. My Wharton buddies dropped me off at the train station; (does anyone really know when to use a semi-colon?) I got on the train and was on my way. At least that is what I thought! As we were approaching the border with Austria, the conductor advised all to prepare their passports for entry into Austria. No problem. I'll just reach into my handy, dandy travel pack, aka, a money belt around my waist. Rut ro....it was not in the usual spot. I tried to recreate (in slow motion, mind you) the same motions involved in the search thinking that somehow the missing passport would appear to me if I looked more deliberately. After a series of consecutively slower and slower searches of all of my belongings, I concluded that my passport had been stolen. It became clear to me that the thieving "elves" who stole it would not return it no matter how slowly I dissected my belongings.

I then reflected on the carefree day that I had spent with a number of my classmates in the Englisher Gartens. It may have been a bit too carefree for me since that is when I must have lost my passport. We had struck up a very friendly relationship with a number of German natives and played a bunch of volleyball with them. When I played volleyball, I did actually leave my money belt—with my passport in it—out of my sight. I believe that was when my passport had been stolen.

I did not fully realize how bad a situation this was. I got to the entry point at the train station in Austria and explained my plight to the guards. They listened politely, and asked again if I had my passport (as if I had not just explained that very point to them!). I replied, "No." They said, "You must go back to the embassy in Germany to get a new passport." I told them that I could not go back as my friends had dropped me off and were then off on a trip up to Berlin. I had no way of rendezvousing with them. I must go forward and meet my friend in Vienna. They said, "No, you must go back."

OK...one more try...let me go REALLY, REALLY slowly through the search this time, because I want to keep as many options open to me to discover where the passport had finally come to rest among my belongings, or at least give enough time for the thieving elves who stole it to return it. I wanted to try to savor the possibility that I might find it this time. Once again, the lack of speed had no impact on the end result. The passport was still gone. And, I was beginning to think...maybe it really was gone. I was pretty slow on the up-take here.

After I completed my final fruitless search, I attempted to use a pay phone to call my friend to let him know that I was stuck at the border and would not be able o meet him in Vienna. For some strange reason, my coins did not work; they were too big for the slots. Then I realized that I was in Austria and my German coins would not work on the Austrian phones. Frustrated by this realization, I headed back to the guard station to seek some help. "The very least THEY could do for me," I thought indignantly, "is allow me to use a phone to call my friend to let him know that I was not coming to Vienna." I approached the guard station where I had been stopped. I was very disappointed, at first, to learn that the guards had disappeared. There was absolutely nobody there to help me...nobody to allow me to use a phone...nobody to help me in any way. There was nobody at the gate from where I had been turned back earlier! Uh...hold on now...that means there is NOBODY to stop me from entering into the country!!! This was not a bad thing...it was a good thing! So I walked past the vacant guard station toward the train platform with a bit more pep in my step. I was going to make it to Vienna after all, I thought.

As I went a little further, I realized much to my dismay, that the entrance to the train platforms that had been open when the guards were at their station, was now closed. My hopes were immediately dashed, at least for a few seconds. Then, I noticed a strange looking device above the two doors to the train platforms. What was it? It sort of looked like a video camera, but it wasn't. What the heck was it? I continued slowly toward the doors to get a closer look at this mysterious electronic device above the doors. As I got closer, I heard a noise, saw some movement and immediately realized what the device was. It was a motion detector that was set to open the doors to the train platform when someone entered the space in front of the doors. The noise and movement was the sound and sight of the "doors to freedom" magically opening before my eyes! I was in range of the motion detector, the doors opened, and I was in!

Once I was on the platform at the station, I became paranoid that I would be discovered. There was no place to hide so I did my best to look like I belonged. Just to increase my cover a little more, in case the guards were walking about the train platform, I huddled up close to an elderly woman so it looked like we were traveling together. I waited for what seemed like a few hours (it was more like 20 minutes) for my train from the border town to Vienna to arrive. As I boarded the train I had one more panicked thought: "What if someone on this train asks for my passport?" Yikes! Was I really free? It seemed like hours before I finally arrived in Vienna (this time it actually was a number of hours).

When I finally connected with my buddy in the Vienna station (which was a lot harder back then with no cell phones), I told him we had to figure out what to do about my passport situation. It was Friday night, and I was scheduled to leave Sunday night on an overnight train to Berlin. We called the US embassy in Vienna just after 5pm on a Friday night. They informed me that the embassy was closed for the weekend so a new passport could not be issued before my departure on Sunday. After some discussion, they said that what I needed to do was go to one of the Tobacco and Stamp stores, and purchase the equivalent of $15 in stamps. Ooooookay, I can do that. But why? Well, Austria is a little funny when it comes to filing police reports. You actually have to purchase these stamps, go to a police station and use the stamps to pay the police to fill out a report that explains that the passport was stolen. That sounded efficient. I asked the embassy representative over and over again, "Are you sure that this is all I need to do to get back into Germany?" I was assured and reassured that the documentation was all I needed.

OK, now that we had settled that problem, I could relax and enjoy Vienna. We did a bunch of sightseeing—mostly bars and cafes. It was really quite beautiful. On Sunday, my friend Steve and I spent most of the day enjoying one of the local parks along with one of the local beers (substitute the word "many" for "one" to be more accurate). It was a really fun day, and towards the late afternoon, it was time to go down to the station for my trip back to Berlin. I had my buddy—who was fluent in German—talk to the people at the station, and on the train, to again ensure that I had everything I needed to get into Germany without a hitch. Once again, everything appeared to be copacetic.

On the train, I ended up in a berth with a friendly German young lady, and her friend. We had a nice time bonding and learning about our respective cultures as the journey progressed. All was going along pretty nicely, until the train approached the border with Germany and one of those conductor-types knocked on the door to our berth and asked for "papers." Papers? Oh, yeah, "papers." I did have papers! I had the papers that the police gave me to report my lost/stolen passport. I confidently gave him my police papers along with my US driver's license, and was immediately relieved that I had taken the time on Friday and then Saturday getting everything I needed for my journey. All was good! I was so relieved that I was going to get to Berlin with no problem; I shared the entire story with my berth mates. They took it all in…and looked hopeful that my plan was fully baked even though I could tell in their eyes that they thought it was barely baked at best.

My euphoria and self-congratulatory moment was rudely interrupted by the conductor who came in, looked at me, looked at my papers, looked back at me and said, "This is no good." Uh, oh… sounds like the plan was only half-baked, after all. By "no good," did he mean that there was some sort of spelling mistake in the paperwork? Was it not a good enough driver's license picture for him to identify me as the person on the "papers?" Well, as it turned out… not exactly. There did not seem to be much room for negotiating. In fact, he seemed pretty definitive. That said, I went through the entire story of my weekend (conveniently leaving out the fact that I had actually entered their country without my passport in the first place).

Now this conductor dude did not speak much English. In fact, I think he knew how to say exactly 9 words. The first four, which he used quite frequently, were, "This is no good." Any guess as to what the other 5 words were? Try this on for size: "You must leave the train." Come to think of it, he used those words a whole bunch, too. I tried to get my berth mates to talk some sense into the conductor in his native tongue. They served as an interpreter both ways. The discussion went back and forth, and back and forth, and finally, just when I thought my pals were making real progress, as the pace and pitch of their arguments started to slow and lower, respectively. Victory was ours! Right? Well… as it turned out… not exactly. The young woman, with much disappointment in her voice said, "I'm sorry, but he insists that you get off the train."

Ugh! I was defeated. I could not talk my way out of this. I collected all of my stuff, bid a fond farewell to my berth mates and then stepped down the steps to the platform at the border to Germany. I walked quickly over to a gathering of border guards and train conductor types who seemed to be having some fun talking with each other. I hated to spoil their "little moment" but I had a bit of an urgent moment of my own. As I approached them, I just prayed that the train behind me would not start rolling on its way to Berlin without me. I needed to do something fast. There were dozens of heads poking out from windows on the train. Each was looking around to see if they could determine the source of this extended delay. Yes… over here… it's me. I'm the reason!

I quickly identified the person I thought was the lead border guard. Coincidentally, he seemed to be the most conversant in English. I went through the entire story from start to finish (again omitting the fact that I had entered Austria without a passport in the first place). Looking at these expensive papers I purchased at the police station with tobacco stamps, he turned to me and said, "This is no good." Two more times, I explained the entire series of events. The final time, I included specific reference to the time I called the embassy on Friday (after 5pm). As I continued on my round of the story, he turned to the other guard, made some sort of comment in German—that must have had something to do with my comment about calling the embassy after 5pm—and then all of the guards started to laugh.

Now I was getting a little annoyed. It was one thing to keep me from continuing on my journey, but it was entirely another to laugh in my face about my plight. Before I could come up with some clever comment to defend my honor, the lead guard, still laughing mind you, handed me my seemingly worthless "papers" and said with a smile, "You may get back on the train." I was stunned, absolutely, stunned. But, as any good salesperson would tell you, stop selling once your customer agrees to buy. No further comment from me, other than a huge and heartfelt, "Thank-you."

I got back on the train, and rejoined my berth mates with some resounding "high-fives," which I realized after their awkward receptivity to my happy, victory ritual, was a completely alien concept to them. I then enjoyed explaining the origin of the "high-five" to my buds.

Once I got to Berlin, I had no clue where to go. I had an address, but no map, no cell phone (they did not exist back then), no GPS...just the kindness of strangers to help me get where I needed to go. Thankfully, the lovely young lady who had tried in vain to defend my right to stay on the train was kind enough to escort me to the hotel I was looking for in Berlin. I think she felt badly for what I had been through, and because it was clear that I had no idea how to get where I needed to go.

After all of this, I finally rejoined my classmates in Berlin and explained my weekend adventure, and the curious interaction that I had on my return trip to Germany at the border with the guards. The very first person that heard the story could not contain his laughter and blurted out, "You are so stupid!" I thought to myself, "While that may be true given what I had gone through—losing my passport and all—I didn't think I deserved to be ripped." He continued, "You are so stupid because you did not realize what they were really asking you for." OK... still not getting it... need a little help over here... maybe I could buy a vowel? So my classmate spelled it out for me quite clearly, "You idiot! You did everything you were supposed to do, but you failed to understand that they were looking for you to give them a bribe in order to get into Germany." Ugh! In retrospect, it was really clear and obvious. And now, I think I have a better understanding of the conversation that the lead guard had with the others just before he allowed me to get back on the train.

I believe the translated commentary probably sounded something like this: "Can you believe this stupid American? He really doesn't get it. All he has to do is give us a little cash, and he's on his way, but he doesn't know that's what we are looking for." Then, I'd like to think that he added the following: "You do have to admire his persistence. Even in the face of an absolute rejection of his plan and his proposed solution to the problem, he continued to try again and again to re-communicate his story in the hopes that some new detail would reveal itself and tip the situation in his favor." Sometimes it is a real advantage to hold your ground, and persist. Sometimes you can even talk your way into a country!

◉ ◉ ◉

**Lessons learned from *Persistence Pays—A Passport: Don't Leave Home Without It!***

◉ **Don't lose your passport**. It is an unbelievable pain/hassle. Every time that I return to the U.S from a trip out of the country. I still get asked about it.

◉ **When you don't give yourself (or have) an alternative to fail, you do what it takes to succeed.** I really had no alternative so I did everything I could do to go forward into Austria and then back to Germany.

⊙ **Persistence pays.** I had no idea what the border guards wanted, so I kept reiterating the only story line I had. Eventually, I wore them down and they allowed me to proceed into Germany without a passport. Innovators need to be persistent in the face of obstacles they may not fully understand.

⊙ **If you act like you know what you are doing, people assume you know what you are doing.** Getting into Austria without a passport was just a bit of luck on my part, but once I was in, I acted like I belonged.

⊙ **Money helps people focus on helping you find things.** I thought it a bit strange that I had to pay the police to write a report that declared my passport stolen. I thought it even more strange that I needed to pay the border guards to accept the police report.

⊙ **Make friends wherever you go.** The people I met on the train helped make my case with the border guards and they helped me find my way to my destination once we made it to Berlin. Treat others how you want to be treated.

⊙ **Corruption does exist, even if you don't recognize it.** I was completely oblivious to the possibility that the border guards may have been looking for a bribe.

# 8 The Less You Know, the More You Can Do... The Power of Inexperience!

This story provides a lesson in the power of inexperience bringing fresh eyes and action to a product category. It is no secret that children are the most creative problem solvers as they lack the experience to know that something cannot be done a certain way. The longer you work in any particular job or industry, the more constrained you become by what you learned. Turn your inexperience into strength by doing what those who are more experienced would dare not attempt.

When I went back to school to pursue my MBA at Wharton I really wanted to learn what it takes to run my own business. That was the reason I drained my 401K, and all of the SB stock that I had socked away in order to help pay for my tuition. As it turns out, my education became a really, really BIG expense as the stock that I had cashed in went up dramatically with the merger of Glaxo and SmithKline Beecham. Oh well. It was worth it. I learned a ton—from the courses and from the other amazing people that I met at Wharton.

One of the more critical steps towards graduation from business school is the summer internship that, for many people, sets the course for what they do after they graduate. I had two things that I was passionate about: entrepreneurship and marketing. As a budding young entrepreneur, the only natural thing for me to do was to seek out a summer job with Wharton's Small Business Development Center (SBDC)—which would have immersed me in the world of start-ups and small businesses. It was exactly what I wanted to do. Unfortunately for me, it was exactly what a ton of other folks also wanted to do.  I wanted desperately to become one of the SBDC consultants, but the consultants they tended to hire all had one thing that I did not—experience as a consultant.  Silly me!  I thought that perhaps my real business experience might be worth a little more than the "advice" that consultants typically sell.  Alas, it did not appear to have much value in the eyes of the people hiring the SBDC consultants.

So what would be a good second choice as a summer internship?  Well, if marketing was my back-up plan, then I might as well pursue the best marketing company I could think of.  P&G had a terrific reputation, but the size of the company was a little bit of a concern for me as I felt like I might get lost in the company.  As a Wharton student exploring summer internship possibilities, I was fortunate enough to be "invited" to take the P&G MAT—which is basically a SAT/GMAT-like standardized test that P&G requires before they interview candidates.  The test focuses on reading comprehension, critical reasoning and math.  Did I mention this is all done before they even agree to interview you?  If you do not meet a certain threshold, then you do not get an interview.  It's that simple.  Fortunately for me, I cleared the P&G MAT hurdle, and went on to the interview stage of the process.

This interview was unlike any other interview I have ever had.  P&G looks for demonstrated leadership from its marketing hires.  They believe that leaders reveal themselves early in life and continue to demonstrate their leadership abilities over time.  In other words, they believe that there is a certain DNA component to leadership that manifests itself over the years with specific examples of leadership.  In a huge stroke of luck, I had a head's up from a buddy of mine that had spent his summer internship at P&G two years prior about the rigorous interview process that was about to unfold.  He told me that I need to have a number of examples of leadership from all stages of my life….and he really emphasized the fact that you need to have a lot of examples. I confidently informed him that I have a couple of great examples, and he said that I'll need 10 times the number of examples I had.

I felt like I was pretty well prepared for the interview. When the questions turned to leadership example, I was ready. I told them about the team that I led at SmithKline Beckman. They asked me for another. I told them how I formed a softball team at SB and recruited people from all over the organization—team Tsunami was the name—before Tsunami. They asked me for another. I told them how I organized the Management Associate Bowlarama. They asked me for another. I told them how I developed an approach to detailing doctors (pharmaceutical speak for selling) that allowed me to achieve call targets and sales results that were unheard of. They asked me for another—but this time one from my college experience. I told them about how I sought out and ultimately got the job as the Anheuser Busch Marketing Representative (that's what I told them the name was…most people would know it is as the "bud man"). They asked me for another. As the Vice President of the Duke Union I oversaw all of the committees responsible for bringing concerts and major speakers, performing arts, galleries and festivals to Duke. They asked me for another. I told them how I was an officer in my fraternity and how much I learned about the "power of the pen" since I was the Recording Secretary responsible for the minutes from the meeting. They asked me for another this time from high school. I told them how I decided to perform stand-up comedy despite every friend and family member trying to talk me out of it. They asked me for another. I told them how I ran for Student Senate and won by the widest margin in the history of the school elections—mostly because I prepared a speech that was equal parts humor and serious. I also talked about how I led a pep rally for the school—which was admittedly a little daunting. They asked me for another this time from middle school. And for the first time, I started to worry that I might not have enough leadership stories ready as I was running on "low." I told them that I was the editor-in-chief for the yearbook for two years and assistant editor for one year. They asked me for another. They asked me for another. I told them how I organized a weekly football competition between my friends in my grade and friends of mine in the grade above. I was tired of hearing people talk about and nothing ever happening, so I made it happen. They asked me for an example from grade school. I talked about how I would organize and lead the formation of kickball teams at recess. Truth be told, I "volunteered" to organize to ensure that my buddies—who also happened to be really good kick ballers—would be on my team. They asked me for another. I told them that after I did not "make" the choir, how I still led the choir by agreeing to be the MC of the show. (Just an aside: how bad is your voice when you get "cut" from the elementary school choir? I tried out for singing and they said, "Hey, how about you introduce the singers!")

Thanks in large part to the advice from my well-informed buddy —part of my network [see Chapter 5 *The Power of Networking*], I felt like I had most of the answers they were looking for. I do confess that the last few were spontaneously recalled as I had not prepared to go so deep into my past despite the forewarning I received. Apparently my trip down memory lane detailing my history of leadership was satisfactory to them. I was offered a job as a summer intern—one of 84 marketing summer interns!! And as an added "small world" bonus, one of my best friends from SmithKline, Jeff Walsh, aka, Walshie, was also going to be at P&G for the summer. This was going to be great!

So I moved into the cozy confines in the Bluffs—in Covington, Kentucky overlooking downtown Cincinnati…along with 10 other summer marketing interns. The fun, the parties and the camaraderie of that group at the Bluffs will be a story for another day (maybe!). The real story was in the learning experience of my summer internship. I was a marketing intern on the Folgers coffee brand team. Many of the folks who worked at P&G in the food and beverage division had clear views about the way that their brands needed to evolve. For the Folgers brand team it was all about building and leveraging the Folgers brand. I was able to come onto the brand team without any baggage about what was "necessary." I was objective and not burdened by the knowledge and experience that people on the brand team had accumulated. I was not constrained by red (caffeinated), green (decaffeinated) and purple (premium blend) can. Knowledge and experience can be a roadblock that prevents you from identifying and pursuing opportunities. Fortunately for me, I had no such knowledge or experience to hold me back. I saw the market for what it was.

My "project" for the summer was to explore the whole bean segment of the coffee category. For the uninitiated, the whole bean segment of the coffee category was in the beginning stages of its massive growth in the U.S. and around the globe. As a point of reference, in the early 90s, Starbucks had 118 stores in the U.S., which is about ½ of the number (255) they have in New York City alone as of 2012. I was "in" on something before it became big. If only I had predicted it and simply invested in Starbucks! Oh, well....

After analyzing the market trends for the coffee category, it was clear that the future growth of P&G's coffee franchise would require them to tap into the fastest growing segment—the whole bean segment. The sales and volume numbers for their regular, decaffeinated, and premium brands were not pretty. Each of those businesses was flat to declining. The category trends painted a similar picture. The overall category was flat but the whole bean segment was experiencing rapid growth. That growth had to come from somewhere. It came from the existing coffee franchises, including P&G's Folgers brand.

One of the more amazing things about the whole bean category was the perception around the coffee "experience." Good marketers know that if you really want to establish a lasting relationship between your brand and your customer then you need to elevate customers to an "experience" with your brand. The whole bean category was all about the "experience." Customers would purchase beans in the supermarket or at specialty stores, and grind them at the store or bring them home to grind them with their own grinders. Finally, they would brew the coffee with the "freshly" ground beans and feel that they just had a wonderful coffee "experience." On top of all of that, consumers happily paid more money to be a part of this experience. In short, they did more work and happily paid for the privilege. Moreover, as a manufacturer in the whole bean category, you do significantly less work—and incur significantly less cost. This sounded pretty interesting... spend less and charge more. Sounded like a winner.

What should Folgers do? Well, for a summer intern who was looking to make his mark in the organization, I thought it was pretty clear. P&G needed to buy their way into the category. It would make little sense (especially to consumers) for Folgers to launch their own line of whole bean coffee. This was a tough pill (or bean as the case may be) for P&G to swallow. They were interested in building around the Folgers brand name. As a relative outsider, however, it was easy for me to see the opportunity, as I was not clouded by the legacy of the Folgers brand. The problem for Folgers was that the "brand" was closely associated with the familiar red (caffeinated), green (decaffeinated) and purple (premium) vacuum-sealed cans of coffee grounds and had little equity to contribute to the whole bean segment. I saw two possible options for P&G:

1. Buy Starbucks—a good option, but not ideal since it would mean buying retail outlets and becoming a retailer.

2.  Buy Millstone (Seattle's Best Coffee)—this was an attractive option as this would allow P&G to get into the whole bean category with a brand that already had a solid reputation, and it fit P&G's business model.

My strong recommendation was that P&G purchase Millstone and keep the brand name. There was much discussion about the potential value of leveraging (or building upon) the Folgers brand and heritage. But at the end of the day, we agreed that consumers would have a hard time with a "Folgers" whole bean entrant.

At the end of my presentation to the Food and Beverage senior leadership team, I got some polite applause (golf claps, of course), and was told that I had done a nice job. I must have been a little persuasive, as P&G purchased Millstone 4 years later. All in a summer's work!

◉ ◉ ◉

### Lessons learned from *The Less You Know, the More You Can Do... The Power of Inexperience!*

◉ **It takes outsiders to see what you cannot.** The internal team could only see things in terms of the current Folgers mix. I was not burdened by this legacy thinking and was able to suggest an approach that seemed to have more connection with consumers while still delivering value to P&G.

◉ **The less you know, the more you can see.** Not being a coffee consumer helped me consider more possibilities.

◉ **Focus on what is meaningful to the consumer first, and your brand second.** Line extensions are not always the answer. In this case, Millstone would not have made sense as a part of the Folgers brand, but it made a lot of sense as a part of P&G.

⊙ **Big companies move slowly.** It took more than 4 years after the initial exploration of the whole bean opportunity for P&G to make their move.

⊙ **Leaders are born and are nurtured over time.** There are some innate leadership skills that you are born with and your experience over time allows you to build on them.

⊙ **Individuals make things happen**. Even in a supremely process-driven organization, the importance of the individual (and the leadership they demonstrate) is paramount. The process is not a substitute for individuals making decisions and taking action.

# 9 | The Power of a Prototype

This story is about the experience I had around another potential innovation when I was a summer intern at P&G. The story will highlight a couple of key points:

> ➢ If customers don't "get it," then you didn't "get it." I had a concept that somehow was invisible to the customers it was intended to serve.
> ➢ Customers can't tell you what to innovate…but they can leave you clues.
> ➢ A prototype communicates more than words can describe.

I already talked about my "major" P&G summer intern project which culminated in a recommendation to the leadership team that P&G purchase Millstone as a way to take advantage of the growing trend towards whole bean coffee. I have not yet discussed an equally important innovation learning experience. I had one of the most brilliant ideas (in my own mind only for those of you keeping score) that I could not wait to pursue. Unfortunately, consumers had a different view of my "brilliance." Their word for it was stupidity.

As a refresher course for those readers with attention deficit, I worked on the Folgers coffee business during my marketing internship. The business was broken down into two distinct categories. Inside P&G, they called it "Red Can" and "Green Can." To the outside world, this was "caffeinated" and "decaffeinated" coffee, respectively.

I was a purist as a marketer on the Folgers brand since I had no love or even like of coffee. There was no risk of confusing me with the coffee customer, or of me mistakenly believing that my views represented those of the customer because I did not like coffee at all. That did not stop me from having opinions and certainly did not stop me from coming up with new business ideas that I felt would rock the coffee world. Remember, I was not "burdened" by experience.

There were a few things that started to become clear to me as I learned more about the coffee category. My "awakening" to the category contributed to the formation of one of the most brilliant ideas that the Folgers brand had ever developed (again, in my mind only). Without further hyperbole, here are some of the interesting category clues:

o Caffeine is a stimulant and will help most people stay alert and awake;
o There are times in the day—usually late at night, when people would enjoy coffee but not the extra "boost" of alertness/wakefulness.
o Caffeine contributes to the flavor of the coffee.
o Decaffeinated flavor is perceived to have less flavor/ strength.
o Decaffeinated drinkers biggest complaint is the lack of strong flavor;
o Coffee drinkers knowingly trade-off flavor for decaffeination;
o The "1/2 Caff" category was becoming increasingly popular as people wanted the combination of a stronger flavor than decaffeinated offered, but did not want the burden of all of the caffeine that went along with it.

Even to the untrained eye, there seemed to be a clear and obvious solution that would revolutionize the coffee category. That's right! It's called "Dial-a-Dose:" a unique coffee dispensing device that allowed customers to dial their own "dose" of caffeine (or flavor) based on their unique preferences. In the morning, customers could go with a fully-flavored and caffeinated dose.   Late morning, they may want to dial it back a little and go ½ caffeinated.  Early afternoon, they might ratchet it up to ¾ caffeinated for that extra boost.  After dinner, they may want to go to 10% caffeinated to give them a little boost, but not enough to keep them up at night.

I know what you are thinking.  I was thinking the exact same thing.  This is awesome.  There seemed to be an opportunity to make money selling the coffee dispensing devices and creating and selling the Red and Green can mini-canister refills. This was the classic razor and razorblade-selling model. The combination of interchangeable canisters would sit side-by-side and allow for quantities of the caffeinated and decaffeinated coffees to be blended easily to meet the customers' preference.  If customers ran out of one of the canisters sooner than the other, they could buy the appropriate replacement canisters.  This screamed of incremental volume!  Did I mention that the canisters would be premium priced?  Man, this idea was getting better and better all the time—as far as I knew.  (Was that what you are thinking?)

Before P&G would allow me to launch this "brilliant" product combination on the market, they did ask me to do them one small favor.  Test it with consumers.  Imagine that!  Did I mention that I am not a coffee drinker?  No problem, I planned to test it with consumers, and just knew that they would love it! We scheduled the focus groups and I have to say there was quite a bit of buzz internally around the potential for this opportunity as we could charge a premium over our existing Red and Green can lines for the convenience of allowing consumers to create their own unique blend.

Before revealing the outcome of the initiative, this might be the appropriate time to point out how difficult it is to get consumers to tell you how they will react to something completely new and different (a little foreshadowing). We learned a lot from those focus groups. We learned that the participants on the other side of the one-way mirrors are in a soundproof room and cannot hear the ramblings, rumblings and grumblings of budding young marketers who are screaming at the focus group participants for their apparent inability to envision a better future for themselves. I felt a little bit like Dustin Hoffman in the scene from *The Graduate* where he is at the back of the church banging on the window trying to change the course of events.... Nobody could hear me as I said, "How do these consumers not understand the benefit to them? What is wrong with them? Who recruited this group? Are they really representative of our potential future customer base?" By the sort of questions I was asking, you probably get the sense for how well my "brilliant" marketing idea was going over with consumers. In short, it was not! They just didn't get it! Damn consumers... getting in the way of an otherwise great innovation!

For P&G, this was a validation of a tried and true marketing methodology. There was a rigorous series of steps that you had to go through before you launch a new product. For me, I had a different take-away: it is really difficult to have consumers react to a concept of some future invention, product or service without a real prototype. I had no prototype. I had a storyboard: a two-dimensional visualization and description of the product and the different situations when consumers might appreciate the caffeine dosing flexibility. If I had produced a prototype of the device, complete with the side-by-side canisters of caffeinated and decaffeinated coffee, this idea would have taken off! There is no doubt in my mind. In fact, it would not surprise me to see that Folgers, or maybe even Maxwell House, now that the cat is out of the bag, decides to launch just such a product. I will gladly accept royalties for the execution of the idea.

⊙ ⊙ ⊙

## Lessons learned from *The Power of a Prototype*

⊙ **Outsiders can sometimes see things more clearly than internal people.** Even still, you need to appreciate the learning and use it to help shape the ideas you pursue.

⊙ **The larger the company, the harder it is to create momentum for change.** Bigger companies require more "proof" before they can support innovation that requires the company to change its way of working.

⊙ **Consumers have a hard time conceptualizing things that do not currently exist.** Consumers cannot tell you exactly what they want, but they can leave you clues. I should have pieced together the clues in a more comprehensible way.

⊙ **You must have a prototype.** A prototype communicates more than words can describe. If I had presented a rough prototype, rather than a picture with a description underneath, consumers would have had a much better understanding of the potential innovation. I goofed!

⊙ **Consumers can be wrong.** They can't tell you what they cannot see and touch. But, they can leave you clues as to their wants and needs.

⊙ **Sometimes you are wrong... but that is how you learn.** This may have been a really bad idea or a good idea poorly executed. In either case, it was my bad.

⊙ **Don't be afraid to try.** There are opportunities everywhere and you can't let fear of being wrong overcome the opportunity to get something right. I still try stuff out all the time.

---

# 10 | It is Not the Idea But the Execution that Delivers Value

This story is about execution. When it comes to creating new value through innovation, it is more about the execution than the idea. Of course, you hope that you have a good idea to start with but there are many great ideas that are squandered in organizations because there is nobody willing or able to do the heavy lifting required to make them happen. In this case, my predecessor handed an idea to me. He started the race, ran the first three legs of the race by himself and handed it off to me to run the anchor leg of the race!

Did I mention that I had a great time in business school and was not overly eager to get back into the real world? I was fortunate enough to get a full-time offer at McNeil Consumer Products, a division of Johnson & Johnson (J&J).

Just after accepting the offer, I asked them when the latest possible start date was. They thought it was a strange question to ask, but I had a lot of things I wanted to do before I got back to the real world and very little time left to do it. I wanted to travel a bit with some of my fellow P&G interns—a few from Kellogg and a few from UCLA. There were 7 of us in total and we had a grand old time traveling to Indonesia and Thailand. It was a fantastic trip that could be the subject of a future book, but, I digress (again). The real point is that when I did finally start my job at McNeil—in September (after graduating from Wharton in May)—there was a collective relief from the folks I was working for. Since I was virtually incommunicado while I was traveling over the summer, they had no idea when (and if) I was going to turn up for my job. I think they may have even had a bet going as to whether I would show up at all. Upon my arrival, I did not actually see any money change hands, but I definitely felt the vibe of "Oh, you finally decided to show up!"

Once I arrived at McNeil, I got right down to business. I joined the TYLENOL Allergy Sinus, TYLENOL Sinus and Sine-Aid brand team as an Assistant Product Director (APD). The people were great, and I was working briefly with a guy who is to this day one of my good buddies—Bob Carpenter (affectionately known as "Bobby C!"). The honeymoon period of my marketing indoctrination did not last long. No sooner did I join the brand, then Bobby C took off to become an APD on the mother ship— Adult TYLENOL. I was left to handle one of the cool innovations that Bob had initiated: the allergy forecast. It may be hard to believe, but back in the early 90s, the concept of an allergy forecast was pretty foreign. The forecast was made possible by a tiny firm in Minneapolis, Minnesota who had a network of manually collected pollen collection devices around the country. It was a tough negotiation with the head of the small pollen forecast company, but eventually we agreed to pay them for the pollen data, which was sent to us in spreadsheets,. We used the data to create a forecast for pollen levels around the country.

The pollen forecast was unique and gave us a platform to create additional value for the brand. I worked with the J&J media department to negotiate an exclusive deal whereby news services (like CNN and USA Today) who wanted to use the pollen forecasts as a centerpiece for their weather programming would feature a banner ad (on TV as this was "pre-internet") for the duration of the forecast. In essence, the brand received free product placement in the form of the banner in exchange for the pollen data we shared with the network. Since the weather forecast ran regularly around the clock, I got "free" media exposure around the clock. Because I was in front of the trend here, we had the exclusive rights to the pollen data. I was able to use this data to help establish the brands credibility in the allergy category. The "TYLENOL Allergy Sinus Pollen Forecast" was a regular feature on CNN's weather segments and USA Today's weather page. It was a nice win for an over-the-counter (OTC) allergy product that was in a battle against the category juggernaut, Benadryl (the market leader).

There was only minor resistance to this innovative approach, because it involved little risk (that's code for "cost") and generated high visibility PR for my brand. Not bad at all. This taught me a really important lesson that I should have known all along. The program was a success because I kept a reasonably low profile along the way. And now the physics of innovation mentioned earlier comes into play: movement causes resistance. The bigger the object or the faster you try to move it, the greater the resistance you will create naturally. The lower profile limited the amount of resistance triggered in the organization.

So what was the real innovation? It was not the idea, per se, as Bobby C conceptualized the idea, and I'm sure he would have driven the opportunity to fruition if he had not moved onto a bigger, more important brand. That said, the value in this innovation was actually getting something done! Doing stuff is what matters. Thinking stuff can be intellectually fulfilling and fun, but doing stuff is where you deliver real value!

**Lessons learned from *It is Not the Idea But the Execution that Delivers Value***

⊙ **Value is created by "doing" things not "thinking" things.** There is usually not a shortage of good ideas to pursue rather there is a shortage of people to deliver the good ideas. Having good ideas is a start but delivering those ideas is where value is created.

⊙ **The "buddy system" works and it goes something like this: "You are on your own, buddy!"** No sooner did I start my job than my mentor left for greener pastures in the organization. Rather than receive thoughtful training, I received the "dump and run." It was nobody's fault, mind you, but definitely was an example of the buddy system at play.

⊙ **Learn fast from those around you as they may not be there very long.** I learned people move around to different jobs frequently and with little warning.

# 11 | Blaze Your Own Trail... Just Because Others Tried and Failed Does Not Mean That You Will

This story is about overcoming the burden of experience to create new value. Often times, people in organizations will try to "help" you understand that you are wasting your time on an initiative because they also had "wasted" their time trying to do something similar. They are just trying to be helpful in guiding you to a better path, but others may be trying to get you off the path because your success would shine a brighter light on their past failure. In either case, the best path forward is to believe in yourself and blaze your own trail!

At this point in my J&J experience, having just launched the TYLENOL Allergy Sinus forecast, I was thinking that this marketing "thing" could be pretty fun. After all, it was pretty cool to try new ways to drive the business. Now, in order to make sense of my inspiration for the next innovation, I need to take you into the way back machine for some details about the experiences that served as the foundation for the opportunity I pursued between Janssen Pharmaceuticals and McNeil Consumer Products both divisions of J&J.

As I mentioned earlier in the book, prior to getting my MBA at Wharton, I had worked as a management trainee at SmithKline Beecham (formerly SmithKline Beckman). After rotating through different business units and functional areas for 2 years, I found myself gravitating to a new group that was being formed in the U.S. pharmaceuticals division called the National Accounts department. This group focused on the emerging purchasing entities that started to exert a fair amount of control over what doctors prescribed. These "entities" were called National Accounts and they included multi-hospital systems, Health Maintenance Organizations (HMOs), and other Managed Care Organizations (MCOs). Interestingly enough, at the time, many people thought that this "managed care phenomenon" would quickly pass. In the world of innovation, you should recognize this reaction as a normal part of the cycle of rejection of all things new. It is perfectly normal to deny the validity of any new solution that challenges the accepted standards of the status quo. Despite all of the denials and non-believers, MCOs have managed to survive and thrive for more than 30 years.

In any event, because these organizations had recently formed and begun enrolling doctors and hospitals into their networks, they began to gain real bargaining power with pharmaceutical companies with regard to the price of prescription drugs. In the early days, the pharmaceutical companies made a mad dash to try and leverage these organizations to their own advantage. The pharmaceutical companies would provide preferred pricing for their prescriptions, in exchange for increased, and in some cases exclusive, access to patients through the managed care controlled formularies.

Working with MCOs was like being in the wild west. Everything was new. There was no precedent for any activity. This was just the way I liked things. Rules were for the other guys. Rules were what prevented other people from doing the sort of high impact things I liked to do. I preferred the wide-open spaces you could only find in new territory, and the National Accounts job was definitely new territory. There was no manual for how we would operate with MCOs...at least initially. Ironically, one of the first things we did was create a manual that showed the process of signing and implementing a National Accounts contract. So much for innovation!

We were making it up as we went but felt it was important to document the process with a manual. It was our way of making our department (and the work we did) seem more "real." We would experiment with programs to try to increase the impact of the contracts that we signed with providers. Some things worked and some things didn't. In the spirit of innovation, we learned along the way. In my brief tenure there, I developed a number of new programs to help our accounts implement the contracts that SmithKline Beecham would sign with MCOs. For example, I developed a marketing program for Kaiser Permanente to help them communicate our brand's presence on their closed formulary. [A closed formulary meant that physicians could only prescribe products that were included on the formulary. The system was closed to products not included on the formulary.]

One of the more important things I learned, and this was by no means Earth-shattering news, was that money matters to these managed care organizations. Yea, that's a real revelation, eh? Money matters! Fundamentally, the only reason that these MCOs and multi-hospital systems existed was because they could leverage scale to exert downward pricing pressure on prescription products. This was their entire reason to be. I also learned that these new organizations really had no interest in spending money if they could avoid it. While on the surface they are purported to be organizations that can improve patient care, in reality, their top priority was to reduce the amount of money they spend on care. This insight gained from my National Accounts experience at SmithKline Beecham helped fuel the partnership opportunity I wanted to develop between McNeil and Janssen.

Now, back to our regularly scheduled J&J innovation story... Even with the allergy forecast providing my brand with positive sales momentum, I needed an encore. TYLENOL Allergy Sinus was the 3rd biggest brand in the allergy category—and very far behind the market leader, Benadryl. I had no interest in a "consolation prize" of 2$^{nd}$ or 3$^{rd}$ in any category. I was determined to find a way to make my brand the #1 brand in the OTC allergy market? I looked around...I tried to figure out what made other brands successful over sustained periods of time. What, for example, allowed the Adult TYLENOL brand to stave off the competitive onslaught of Advil, Motrin, and generic forms of acetaminophen? One of my observations was that the professional heritage (e.g. extensive use in hospitals and physician endorsement) had helped the Adult TYLENOL brand defend against numerous competitive threats. The "halo effect" of TYLENOL's endorsement by doctors was huge! I honed in on that point as the starting point of my innovation efforts. I concluded that my brand's future depended on professional endorsement. I simply had to get doctors to endorse/promote my brand to their patients suffering from allergies. "If the Adult TYLENOL franchise could do it," I rationalized, "why couldn't I?"

Let me take a crack at answering my own question. Well, for starters, the Adult TYLENOL brand had two things that I did not: a professional sales force and money. Other than that, we were very similar. [Reminds me of one of my favorite elephant jokes: What are the similarities between an elephant and a plum? Answer: They are both purple—except for the elephant!] Except for the money and sales force, we were the same! That said, there was no way I could afford to build or even rent a comparable professional sales force. So how could I attain the professional endorsement I sought without spending any money? I was not the market leader. Benadryl was. I did not have money to invest in a professional sales force. I was willing to invest the limited funds I did have in samples and coupons for consumers, but again, I did not have a mechanism to get these samples/coupons to physicians and their patients. What to do? What to do? I felt like Winnie-the-Pooh when he jabs his finger against his head over and over again as he implores himself to "Think, think, think, think!"

And then it struck me. My years of toil dealing with managed care organizations at SmithKline Beecham was about to pay off. MCOs would LOVE to promote an over-the-counter allergy product to their patients who are suffering from allergies. If the product worked, then there would be no cost to the MCO. This was a reasonable hypothesis but I still had a major problem. I had no sales force to get my message to physicians and test my hypothesis. "Wait a minute," I thought. Janssen Pharmaceuticals (another J&J company) does have a professional sales force and they have an allergy product— Hismanal—that is struggling for market share against the market leaders—Seldane and Claritin. It's so simple! I'll just ask them to distribute my samples and coupons for me. After all, we are all part of the same family, right? They are also a J&J company and should be motivated to help drive the success of their sister company and brand. For those of you who have not worked in large corporations, you may have missed the very obvious sarcastic undertones of my last statement. Company divisions within corporations always support the success of other divisions… only if it is in the best financial interest of their particular division.

I talked it over with some of my colleagues, including my boss. The reaction was a typical reaction to something new: "Bad idea! Don't waste your time! We've tried numerous times to do something with 'those people' at Janssen and it never led to a productive outcome." Part of this reaction was due to the past failures of those senior leaders in trying to negotiate agreements with other divisions of J&J—including Janssen.

Some of my peers were even more visceral in their objection. "We are a consumer products company. What could you possibly gain from working with a pharmaceutical company?" I also received the "not-so-subtle" message that my plan lacked an obvious benefit to the Hismanal brand—which would usually be followed by "you idiot." I was essentially asking their sales force to promote my less potent allergy OTC brand over their prescription brand to doctors. What would Janssen have to gain by supporting a selling proposition of OTC TYLENOL Allergy Sinus (TAS) as first line therapy followed by HISMANAL as second line therapy?

To answer this question, let's look at things from Janssen's perspective. Hismanal was a distant 3rd in an allergy category dominated by two market leaders. For those of you who need a lesson in business, it is usually not a good idea to be the 3rd horse in a two horse race. Try to be one of the first two horses if you can. If you can't be one of those two, then you need to do something different to get yourself back into the race. For HISMANAL, the race was becoming more challenging since MCOs were increasingly questioning whether HISMANAL even belonged on their formulary. MCOs were under a lot of pressure to include only the top two branded products on formulary in a given category. In essence, the MCOs controlled physician and patient access to HISMANAL. If the brand is not on formulary, then the HISMANAL prescription cannot be filled as written and would be switched to one of the two leading competitors. Formulary access was the major problem that my solution would address.

In order to give HISMANAL a "reason to be" on the MCO formularies, we had to come up with something that was of interest to them. That is where the "unique selling proposition" of OTC first line therapy, and prescription second line therapy came into play. From our earlier discussion, we know that money seems to be pretty important to MCOs (please note the subtle hint of sarcasm). HISMANAL's National Accounts team had already negotiated favorable pricing that should have moved the sales needle within the organizations. There was not much interest from Janssen in further reductions in their pricing. They were interested in exploring opportunities that did not involve pricing.

So along came me and my brand with an interesting proposition. What if we go to MCOs as a "package" deal? We promote TAS as the FIRST line therapy for patients who suffer from allergies. If TAS did the trick, the patient is happy, and the MCO is happy—no cost to them. If the first line therapy does not work, then the physicians—according to the formulary—are to use HISMANAL as the 2nd line therapy. In support of the program, Janssen's sales representatives would agree to distribute samples, distribute TAS coupons, and promote this unique treatment approach for TAS and HISMANAL. The cost of the OTC brand was typically less than the cost of a co-pay for one of the Rx brands, so if the patient used my OTC brand, then they would spend less money to resolve their condition. The MCOs would also spend less money since they pay nothing to support the purchase of OTC brands by their patients. This innovative managed care partnership had the potential to get Hismanal back in the race by increasing their access to managed care formularies.

Now, let's just see if this innovative program passed the "What's In It For Me" test. I could clearly see what was in it for the patient and MCO as it lowered their cost of successful treatment if my OTC brand worked. For Janssen, the program increased formulary access to HISMANAL across multiple MCOs—which meant that patients could get the product as prescribed by the physician. This was huge since prescriptions can only be fulfilled if the product is on the MCO formulary. For the MCOs, the program lowered their cost of treatment. If doctors recommended that patients try TYLENOL Allergy Sinus as their first line therapy, then the MCO would pay nothing. Only if the patient failed on the first line therapy would the physician then write a prescription for HISMANAL. This was a win all the way around.

What were the results of this cross-company partnership? The Janssen sales representatives helped establish TAS as a serious player in the allergy market with their promotional activity. My brand gained an implied professional endorsement by physicians who distributed samples and coupons to their patients suffering from allergies. In essence, I had the benefit of a professional sale force supporting my business, and none of the cost. This program also helped drive impressive sales growth of +35%. For Hismanal, the program increased formulary coverage and gave the brand a "reason to be" in a very competitive category.

As I recall and write down the details of this idea for this book, I admit that I see some of the wisdom of my skeptics (warning: the more you learn and experience, the less open to new ideas you become). Fortunately for me, I had no such wisdom at the time (code for I did not know any better), so I believed this was a great idea! I was not burdened by my experience. At the time, I had relatively little actual business experience so I was stupid enough to believe that I could actually overcome the problems that stood in the way of success. I would not take no for an answer. When I heard no, I interpreted it as "know," as in "they don't know what I know, and if they did, they would say yes." Call it what you will: stubborn, tone-deaf or maybe all deaf, but when someone says no to me, I take it as a sign that I have not done a good enough job of communicating what I know. Oddly, my lack of experience helped turn me into an effective catalyst and champion for this opportunity. I inadvertently created a new innovation corollary: "The more you know, the less you see (vision). The less you see, the less you do." Fortunately for me, I was not burdened by knowledge!

Somehow, this cross-company partnership survived a persistent chorus of naysayers who constantly reflected on the past failed attempts at internal partnerships. The key was to identify the specific value for all partners. To persevere in this environment, you need to recognize that the past does not predict the future. You would not drive a car on a highway looking in the rear-view mirror to navigate the path forward. You would hit a lot of stuff along the way and probably crash. Likewise, you cannot advance your business forward by constantly looking at the past. Some say that if you do not learn from the past you are doomed to repeat it. The key is to learn why something has failed and do it differently in the future. It could have been the wrong time, place, people, or iteration of the idea that led to the failure. Learn and advance into the future. Don't live in the past. Blaze your own trail.

The other critical reason for the success of the partnership was my partner on the Janssen side. Fortunately for me, I had the opportunity to work with someone at Janssen who was extremely progressive and embraced the opportunity from the start. There is no way that this program could have happened without the efforts of my partner at Janssen, Alex Gorsky, who undoubtedly had to face even more significant questions and obstacles than I did. He was able to battle through his own chorus of doubters in order to make this program work. By the way, my partner at Janssen managed to continue on a very successful career path. I'm not going to claim that our joint campaign was the catalyst to his meteoric ascension. It could just be a coincidence that he quickly rose through the management ranks at J&J, then Novartis and is currently back at J&J as the CEO. Just sayin'! ☺ Me? I'm writing this book. Some meteor, eh? Or is this another example of the elephant joke playing out? We are both CEOs of multi-billion dollar global companies...except for me.

**Lessons learned from *Blaze Your Own Trail...Just Because Others Tried and Failed Does Not Mean That You Will***

⊙ **Focus on the ways it can be done!** There are always a million good reasons why something can't be done. Acknowledge that impossibilities exist, then focus on the ways it can be done. Don't accept past failures as an excuse.

⊙ **You don't get if you don't ask!** If you don't ask someone to partner with you, the answer is no. If you ask, the answer could be yes. Ask!

⊙ **Don't let your experience (or the experience of others) blind you to opportunities.** The more you know the less you see. The less you see the less you do. There were many others who had experienced failed partnerships within J&J and they felt obliged to view the opportunity through that lens.

⊙ **Just because others failed, doesn't mean you will.** Many factors could have led past initiatives into failure—wrong time, place, people, etc. Learn what you can from past failures and make it happen.

⊙ **Leverage your past learning and experience to solve new problems.** I saw an opportunity to leverage my managed care experience to create value for my brand through a partnership with another J&J division.

⊙ **It is easier to succeed when everyone has a stake in the success.** Focus on what is best for all parties involved. I was fortunate enough to develop a value proposition that was attractive to the patient and the payer as my OTC product cost patients less than the typical co-pay for a prescription, and cost payers nothing. And of course, I made sure that I delivered something of value to my trusted partner at Janssen.

⊙ **Follow the money trail as it drives behavior.** The payers were motivated by the prospect of addressing the medical need at no cost to them. Money matters most.

⊙ **Be persistent.** Your priority is unlikely to be the top priority of any potential partner until you have had the opportunity to build the relationship and tell your story—again and again and again.

⊙ **Don't take no for an answer.** Make it happen. Rise above the obstacles that are a normal part of driving anything new in organizations.

# 12 | Find Opportunities in Other People's Trash

This story is about seeing what others often overlook and the challenges of establishing external partnerships to help drive your business. You can learn a lot from what others discard as "trash." When I was working on the TYLENOL Sinus brand, there was an innocuous-looking package that was circulated through the marketing department. Many people looked at it for what it was. I looked at it for what it could be for me and my brand in the future and that made all the difference. Think for yourself, try to make a connection to your business, and most importantly, do something! Here is the story…

In keeping with the same approach towards innovation I took with TYLENOL Allergy Sinus, I sought a partner who could provide me with a professional endorsement "halo" for TYLENOL Sinus. Once again, I had no sales force and no budget to build a sales capacity. Furthermore, J&J had no sinus-related products on the professional side in any of its other divisions, so I would not be able to piggyback on the efforts of a sister company. What to do? I needed to find a sales force to distribute my samples and coupons to physicians outside of J&J. I honestly had no idea where to start.

Every now and then sales representatives would come across interesting things and send them into marketing to let us know what is happening out in the "real" world. This helped the marketers stay up-to-speed with what is going on in the front lines, and it was also the way that sales reps let "inside" folks know that they exist. It gets them on the internal radar.

One of those interesting things that was being passed around happened to be a sinusitis kit that Eli Lilly had developed in support of its Lorabid product (a prescription strength sinusitis brand). It was passed from Group Product Director to Product Director and finally to lowly Assistant Product Director—little old me! It was just sitting there…an opportunity waiting to be discovered. It was one of those things that make you go: "Huh!" And that is "Huh" in the interesting sense, not "Huh?" in the questionable sense—just to be clear. Inside the kit was a pamphlet, which felt more like a book, on the symptoms of sinusitis and some of the treatment options. Also included in this kit were a sample and a coupon for one of the 3$^{rd}$ tier over-the-counter (OTC) sinus medications, Bayer Sinus. Surprisingly, it was not the 800-pound gorilla Sudafed that I would have expected to be in this sort of professional package.

I have to admit that I took our exclusion from the kit personally and this drove me to action. I was shocked that a third tier brand had a spot that was rightfully mine. I really felt that way. I was outraged actually. What self-respecting Product Manager at Eli Lilly (in their right mind) would want a third-tier sinus player when they could benefit from the fastest growing OTC sinus product in the category—TYLENOL Sinus? I felt insulted that Eli Lilly had not reached out to me in the first place.

So, what was I to do with this "new information?" I could have done what most people do which is to do nothing and assume that if there were an opportunity here somewhere then my enlightened leaders would certainly let me know. After all, isn't that what leaders do? Or, I could do something for myself as this was my space and my brand could benefit from some form of partnership here. Maybe this was the way that I could again get the halo of professional endorsement for my brand on someone else's dime.

I soon came to grips with the fact that as much as I had wished I were, I simply was not the center of the universe for brand directors at Eli Lilly. In fact, I was pretty certain at this point that he had no idea who I was. I realized it was up to me to make myself known to the unsuspecting product director of Lorabid. Once known, I stood a much better chance of getting to his center of the universe and supplanting my competitor's product in the next set of Lorabid Sinusitis Kits being assembled and distributed by Eli Lilly. I really believed that this could be a great opportunity for TYLENOL Sinus to move into Lilly's patient/physician Sinusitis starter kit. That was the plan.

Support? Did I have any support for my little private war? Well, there was not outright rejection—which in the world of innovation translates to "enthusiastic support" in my book. There were some naysayers who felt that it could potentially be a lot of work and could yield nothing. Once they understood that the additional work would be my own, the resistance waned. It is a shame that the operating principal of far too many people is that they make decisions based on certainty of success. They don't want to expend ANY effort unless there is a guarantee that their time will be rewarded. Innovation doesn't work that way. It is replete with uncertainty.

From the Lilly perspective, I had to consider what was in it for them and address it in my approach. By taking the first critical steps towards doing something and bringing my Lilly partner value, I discovered more things that I needed to know in order to succeed. Innovation is always a work in process. The key is to get the work started. The secret that innovators and entrepreneurs know is that there is no way to predict what you will learn and what mid-course adjustments are therefore required to achieve success. There is no certainty. The only way to find the right course is to start "doing stuff." You must learn by doing, not by thinking. Don't get me wrong, there is a very useful role for analysis, but it should never be an excuse for inaction or unnecessary delay.

I didn't really ask anyone for permission to initiate this partnership with Lilly. I merely informed my boss that I was planning to get free distribution of coupons and samples to physicians and sinusitis sufferers and that I would not have to pay anything other than the cost of shipping the samples to Lilly. That seemed to work. Low risk (cost) creates less resistance.

I knew what I wanted to do... I just needed to go do it. I called directory assistance (Does anyone even know what that is anymore?) for the main telephone number of Eli Lilly in Indianapolis, then called, got transferred around a few times before finally connecting with the Product Manager on Lorabid. It took awhile. Actually, it took a few days to get to the right person, but then we were talking. I first asked what relationship they had with my competitive OTC brand and he responded that it was not a deep relationship. I then mentioned that TYLENOL Sinus was the #2 selling and fastest growing OTC sinus product in the market. I suggested that being associated with such a rapidly growing brand would create a positive halo for Lorabid (magnanimous me thinking only of my partners best interest!). I also indicated that TYLENOL was the #1 product for headaches and other pains and that there was a huge % of sinus sufferers who also suffered from headaches. TYLENOL Sinus made a lot of sense for Lorabid...much more than my competitor.

After a couple of conversations, and some shared logistical information, we agreed to send TYLENOL Sinus samples and coupons to Lilly. The coupons and samples were then inserted into the sinusitis kits and distributed to physicians across the country by another company's sales representatives. What did this distribution cost me? Nothing! It would cost me absolutely nothing other than the time to build the relationship with the Product Manager at Lilly, and the cost of shipping the samples and coupons.

The TYLENOL Sinus/Lorabid partnership helped the business grow at a record pace (+30%). We did not have a professional physician-focused sales force nor did we have the resources to build one. This is an important point as I was trying to achieve professional endorsement, and seemingly, I had no good options. On paper, this situation was what people refer to as a "non-starter." Can't be done! It's clear that there was no way to get to my goal from where I was... unless I believed I could.

I guess you could argue that it was serendipitous that the Lorabid Sinus kit was circulating at the very moment that I was exploring potential avenues to gain professional endorsement. I think there is more to it than that. I think there is a DNA component that drove me (and drives other innovative types) to embrace something new. This is the "I" in innovation. The "individual" is critical to the success of innovation. I don't know if it is the "thrill of the ride," but I am so much more energized when trying to blaze new trails than when I am continuing down a proven path. Maybe it is the risk that triggers some adrenaline, or maybe it is the satisfaction of doing what others do not think possible. In any event, I find doing the impossible a whole lot of fun…so much so…I try to do it everywhere I go.

⊙ ⊙ ⊙

**Lessons learned from *Find Opportunities in Other People's Trash***

⊙ **Opportunities are all around you.** Observe and apply to your business. This one was just sitting around waiting to be discovered and acted upon. Don't accept your observations as confirmation of the status quo, but as a sign of what the future could be for you.

⊙ **Have a clear goal.** In this case, I wanted professional endorsement for my brand for free. This clear goal colored the lens through which I saw things, and as a result I saw the Lorabid kit as a huge opportunity. It fit perfectly. I just needed to convince the Lorabid brand team to "sub" me in, and take my competitor out.

⊙ **Thinking isn't doing...doing is doing!** Thinking does not get anything done. You need to make things happen. I could have continued to be consumed by the "tyranny of the urgent" and rationalized that I had no time to get distracted by a new potential opportunity. Instead, I chose to do something.

⊙ **Anything is possible if you make it in the best interest of another.** To get what you want in a partnership, you need to focus on what others want first. This is the concept of a "value exchange." To get something of value from someone, you need to give something of value to them first.

# 13 | Operate Without a Safety Net

Too often, we rely on the wisdom of others (usually our boss) to guide us to the right decision. In many ways, we rely on leadership as our "safety net" to catch us if we stumble and fall. This story highlights the importance of operating as if you had no safety net in order to make the best decisions and do your best work.

In addition to having fun with new approaches to the TYLENOL Allergy Sinus (TAS) and TYLENOL Sinus (TS) businesses (as discussed in Chapters 11 and 12), I also had responsibility for SineAid. One of my fellow Assistant Product Directors on TYLENOL Sinus and SineAid left the brand and my boss went on maternity leave. I was left running 3 brands with collective revenue of nearly $100M. Not a bad opportunity for someone who was less than one year out of business school. I had the great "pleasure" of putting together 3 business plans. Most other brands had a team of people working on one brand alone. I had a team of brands being worked on by me alone! It was a ton of work, but it taught me a lot in a very short period of time. I quite enjoyed the feeling of running the businesses myself. That's why I went to business school in the first place— to run my own business and be accountable for my success or failure. And there I was doing it...sure I was part of a much bigger organization, but it felt like I was running my own business.

A key part of running these business was launching new products. I was in the midst of launching a number of new products and extensions across my brands, including: TAS Geltabs and Gelcaps, TS Geltabs and Gelcaps, and TYLENOL Severe Allergy (TSA). The latter was an entirely different product and formulation—using a more powerful antihistamine, diphenhydramine. I was jamming. And I was in charge (for you old-timers, it was sort of like how Secretary of State Al Haig thought he was in charge under President Ronald Reagan—I may have thought I was more in charge than I actually was). I was getting stuff done and making things happen. Then, a funny thing happened. The company brought in a new Product Director, Peter Luther, and Group Product Director, Mitch Walker as my new boss and boss's boss respectively. I respected and got along well with both of them, but it was strange "suddenly" having two layers of management that I was unaccustomed to having previously.

I had become accustomed to being the person responsible for making the decisions on the brand and appreciated the freedom (and pressure) associated with making the "call." I was never someone who liked being told what to do in almost any circumstance or situation. I like to figure things out for myself. If I lacked experience in a certain area, I would make up for it with an abundance of confidence. I might make a mistake here and there, but I quickly adapt and make the appropriate course corrections.

So now that I had a few layers of management reinserted into the picture, I still felt confident to make the decisions but I immediately felt like the final say did not rest with me. Keep in mind, that neither Peter nor Mitch had said anything to me about any changes to the decision-making process. I simply assumed that they were now in charge and allowed myself to become somewhat deflated as a result of this self-perceived "demotion."

When Peter and Mitch entered the management picture, I was very close to the all-important "go/no go" launch decision on the TYLENOL Severe Allergy product. Ultimately, I needed Mitch to sign off on the launch of this product. Again, I assumed that he was now the man in charge of the business and the decisions. I presented the rationale and support for the launch and asked him what he would like to do. He asked me what I would like to do. I thought he was just being respectful to the work I had done on the project and ultimately that he would make the call. I told him, "It's not up to me, it is up to you." He turned the tables on me. He said, "If it were up to me, I would not launch the product, but it is up to you. You convinced me that you know more about this product, the category and the customer than I do. It is up to you."

Wow! I was stunned, so much so that I actually hesitated, as I was expecting him to make the call. Was he playing some sort of Jedi mind trick on me? This was all so baffling. As much as I always wanted to make the call, I did not really believe that I was going to be allowed to make it. I assumed the safety net of management oversight had been put back in place when Mitch arrived. When full permission—and responsibility—was reaffirmed, I must admit that I had to do a quick mental inventory of all of the things that could potentially go wrong. He was really going to let me make the call. After re-gathering my senses and coming to grips with the fact that I was operating without a safety net, I concluded that my original instinct was solid. I decided to launch the product. I still could not believe that he let me make the call.

So, I had to ask him his rationale for letting me do something that he did not agree with. He reiterated his belief that I knew more about the launch than he. He also said that my passion for and conviction about this opportunity made him comfortable allowing me to make the call. He then asked me what I thought the worst-case scenario was. Before I could answer, he interjected that the company might lose a few million dollars and I would be all the wiser as a marketer as I learned something that only comes with experience. Wow! Who thinks like that? Mitch did. I'll never forget that lesson in "learning by doing."

Truth be told, in retrospect, I think I might have made the wrong call. The product successfully generated millions in incremental sales for McNeil but it could have done better. I went to market with a "severe" allergy product on the strength of a stronger antihistamine (the allergy medicine). I should have also included an additional ingredient that would have allowed us to claim that it treats more conditions peripherally related to allergies. I was thinking too purely about the "severe allergy" name. To me, severe allergy meant stronger allergy. I think I fell in love with my own plan a little too early and was not as open to those who suggested that we look at a multi-symptom play vs. a stronger allergy play. The rationale for this combination of ingredients was simple: it treats more symptoms—not just allergy symptoms. The multi-symptom play likely would have generated more business for the company. What I did was not bad, per se, but could have been better. Lesson learned!

## Lessons learned from *Operate Without a Safety Net*

⊙ **Learn by doing.** My boss recognized something that was a critical part of my growth as an innovator and as a leader. You learn much faster by doing things. Right or wrong, you need to take action in order to learn. And the best way to learn is to do it without the safety net of different levels of approval that are there to prevent you from making mistakes.

⊙ **Operate your business as if it were your own.**  There is no safety net of a boss who will shield you from the outcome of your decisions.  Make your decisions as if you had no safety net.

⊙ **Don't fixate on your own plan**.  Listen to others who may have insight relevant for your innovation.  In my case, I could not hear any of the fans of the "multi-symptom" product as I was fixated on the "stronger allergy" product.

⊙ **Passion sells.**  Others will look to you for permission to believe in your idea or innovation.  Your passion can help to overcome obstacles that would otherwise prevent you from succeeding.

⊙ **Leaders can help push innovators.**  Belief is inspirational.  The fact that my boss believed enough in what I was doing to allow me to make the launch decision inspired me.  I really felt an entirely different sense of ownership and accountability because he empowered me.  I wanted to do what I believed was right, but I had an extra incentive to do it right because he believed in me.  I did not want to let him down.

# 14 | Shamelessly Steal!

The phrase "shamelessly steal" may sound bad but it is simply an alternative way of expressing the concept of sharing best practices around the organization. Rather than say, "Let's share best practices" we say "shamelessly steal" the best practices for our team. I assure you that it does not involve "stealing" any intellectual or physical property. In keeping with my tendency to take experiences in one field and apply them to another, I developed a best practices "innovation" during my days at J&J. To tell this story, I need to back up a little. Between my first and second year at Wharton, I had the privilege of working as a marketing intern at Proctor and Gamble. I later learned that some, in Cincinnati, referred to the company as Proctor and God—in reverence, not to be blasphemous. So I guess in some ways I stole something from the gods. Here is the story...

Working at P&G that summer was a lot of fun on a number of levels. First, I was born in Cincinnati and YES to the next natural question...my dad did work at P&G at the time—where else would he work in Cincinnati? Anyway, back to the story... the second benefit of my P&G experience was the appreciation it provided me for the power of process. P&G is known for their emphasis on process. People are nice but process is better because it is scalable! One of my keen observations about the people at P&G was there seemed to be a lot of ex-military people. Why is that? It is because they are very accustomed to, and comfortable with, following orders (aka, "the process"). I, on the other hand, find the concept of conformity and following orders utterly repugnant...but that's just me.

My inner "rebelliousness" probably contributed to the role I ended up playing in a summer intern project. I starred in the video production of *Ivan the Intern* that helped give potential future summer interns a flavor for the marketing intern experience at Procter and Gamble. This video became a long-lasting tribute to my summer intern experience as it was showcased at business schools the following recruiting season. My character relished the opportunity to poke fun at the various idiosyncrasies within the culture. The story was based on actual events experienced by yours truly, but naturally, we changed the names to protect the innocent.

One of the more amusing story lines revolved around the enormous "satisfaction" that one can achieve in producing a beautifully written one-page memo. For those uninitiated into the ways of P&G, this is one of their more famous contributions to business norms. The goal was to make the memo so clear and compelling that anyone coming off of the street would be able to understand the recommendation and the supporting rationale. Undaunted, I undertook the challenge to crank out my one-page memo in record time. And I probably would have had the record if it weren't for a "few" revisions with little "nits" (a P&G term for suggested improvements) from my boss. Now, this memo did go through a number of minor iterations, mind you. Those iterations and revisions lasted nearly 8 full weeks! But I can tell you this with some authority...THAT one page memo was absolutely KILLER! Clear, concise, and impactful! It was all there: Background, Recommendation, Key Learnings, Conclusions, and Indicated Actions. I had given birth to the killer memo AND the main story line for the video!

While you may feel that I am being a bit dismissive of the process to develop this succinct memo, nothing could be further from the truth. Yes, it did take a long time for me to figure out that I did not need a lot of flowery prose cluttering up an otherwise clear communication, but once I got it down, I used this model over and over again quite effectively. Like many things, the learning part was a little painful, but the benefit of the learning has been immeasurable. This framework for a memo was one of the things I shamelessly stole from the gods of marketing.

I had a lot of fun working with a few other interns to memorialize the one-page memo "experience" in the video we produced. *Ivan the Intern* became an unexpected smash hit on the business school circuit for the next few years. P&G executives used it to show the more human side of their culture and to attract potential interns and employees.

The final thing P&G did really well was focus on continually training its people. In addition to learning the art of the one-page memo, and how to produce a video, I did learn a lot about the process of evaluating advertising copy during my internship. This is one of the things that P&G prides itself on and they take their copy development process very seriously. Copy development is not some dressed up way of saying I know how to use a Xerox machine to make copies (please insert "canned" laughter here so you know it is OK to laugh). Copy development is the process you go through to develop persuasive advertising (the copy) for consumers.

As part of the copy development training, P&G ran copy lunches each month. A reel of P&G advertisements ran in the lunchroom and the marketers would take turns analyzing what they liked or did not like about the copy. Each marketer would start by sharing their "gut" reaction to the copy and then break it down to understand why they felt that way. The most junior people would comment first and then comments would work their way up to the most senior marketers. It was a great process for learning.

Now let's fast forward to my J&J marketing experience. I was happily working at J&J and found myself longing for an opportunity to bond with my colleagues while learning the fine art of "copy development." Boom! It hit me! Let's do the same thing at J&J that I did at P&G. The biggest expense on most of our brands was advertising copy development and the media expense to support the ads once developed. It was really important to have skill in developing great ads. Why not borrow again from the gods of marketing and shamelessly steal the copy lunch idea from P&G and apply it to McNeil?

I decided to create a reel of the best advertisements and then create a lunch forum for the rest of the Assistant Product Directors (APDs), and Product Directors (PDs) to attend. Great idea, right? Well, that all depends on your perspective. If you were another APD or PD, you might be tempted to avoid or even sabotage this version of a PD Forum. Why? (Please refer to my earlier story about corporate antibodies in Chapter 2). Because if it is a success, then someone else looks good (the initiator) and that may inadvertently make others (the resistors) look bad, at least in a paranoid sort of way. I know that sounds strange but it is the way that people think.

I quickly got the support of the VP of Marketing, Tony Vernon, who thought it was a great opportunity to improve our copy development skills while also building a stronger team who would feel more comfortable collaborating on different marketing-related issues.

One of the keys to introducing new things into organizations, as I have come to learn, is to have the appropriate senior executive supporter on-board (see Tailbrands and Campus Consumer stories in Chapters 22 and 24, respectively). In this case, the fact that the VP of Marketing supported the effort was noteworthy. What actually put us over the top however was the free lunch that went along with the PD Copy Lunch sessions. Oh, and did I mention that Tony agreed to kick off the first PD

Copy Lunch himself? I'm pretty sure that contributed to the perfect attendance across all of the PD and APD ranks.

While the VP of Marketing was a key driver of initial attendance, the free lunches and the fun learning environment we created kept people coming back for more. Month after month we would have our reviews of advertising copy and people at all levels would have the opportunity to share their views and gain further experience in the art of copy development. A by-product or "collateral benefit" of these well-attended sessions was that there was a big increase in the amount of collaboration among the people across all of the brands. I believe this learning forum still operates within McNeil today.

### Lessons learned from *Shamelessly Steal!*

⊙ **Apply learning from one environment to another (this is what is called "shamelessly stealing").** In this case, I had an experience at P&G that I thought could be valuable if applied to J&J. I could have been wrong, but it did not stop me from trying.

⊙ **Gain senior executive support.** The support of the VP of Marketing was critical to allow for the foundation of the Copy Lunches to be built. I have no illusions over motivation for attendance early on. People attended because it was important to the VP. Thereafter, people came back because there was something in it for them (a free lunch and learning).

⊙ **Try to gain grass roots support from those impacted.** I had reached out to a number of different PDs and APDs to have them lead portions of the meetings as they saw fit. This was important to make people feel that it was their meeting, not mine.

⊙ **Expect resistance.** As with anything new, there will be resistance and you should expect it, not be stopped by it. It was easy for some PDs and APDs to resist before the sessions began, but once people learned that it was a valuable use of time, resistance faded.

⊙ **Give people permission to believe in the project.** In the face of resistance, people will look to the initiator for signs of strength or weakness in the face of resistance. You need to give them the show of strength behind your belief in the program. If you believe, they will believe...eventually.

⊙ **Free food is a good thing!** Don't underestimate the power of a free lunch to attract an audience. It may sound like a gimmick, but if the gimmick works, then it is a great strategy.

# 15 | Look Before You Leap!

This story is a lesson in looking before you leap. I was so interested in doing "my own thing" that I fell in love with the idea of starting this cool business within SmithKline Clinical Laboratories. I did not dig deep enough into the opportunity because I really wanted it to be what I hoped it could be. I conveniently overlooked or rationalized many of the troubling signals I did receive and failed to recognize the opportunity for what it actually was. I also did one of the things that you are told never to do...take a job based on a person you know. I happened to know the VP of Sales and Marketing really well and was looking forward to working with him. That relationship was a big factor in my decision to leave J&J. Here is the story...

I was happily working at J&J when Don Hardison, a friend/colleague from my SmithKline days, called me to talk about an opportunity that he was working on at SmithKline Clinical Laboratories (SBCL). They were planning to build a point-of-care (POC) testing business and needed someone with a business background to come in and help them build it. The device they envisioned would do the top 50 most-requested tests at the point-of-care at the bedside of patients in hospitals with just a drop of blood. The test results would be available in minutes. Once the results were delivered, the doctor could make the appropriate clinical decisions for on-going care. This platform had the potential to improve the quality of care by reducing the length of stay (and cost) for patients in hospitals as the test results and the appropriate care would be immediately administered.  SBCL had all of the R&D people they needed to get this project going, but really needed a commercial business leader.

This sounded like the right opportunity at the right time.  I had just done a number of really cool things at J&J in a little over 18 months and had a strong taste of leadership given I had run 3 businesses totaling more than $100M all by my lonesome self.  As I mentioned previously, it was a ton of work, but I loved the feeling of autonomy and accountability.  Once the management vacancies above me had been filled, the job became less interesting to me as the scope of the work reverted back to tasks typically done by Assistant Product Directors.  I had a taste of greater responsibility and I liked it.  I was yearning for more.

After 14 months in my J&J marketing role, I got my first symptoms of a condition that I have termed, "early-onset-job-ADHD."  This condition has a way of changing the perception of the afflicted business person regarding their relative interest in their current role/job.  Opportunities and responsibilities that would otherwise be interesting and maybe even exciting when new, quickly fall out of favor and become the source of mild discontent that festers until the afflicted changes jobs.  That is when I start to look for the shiny new penny (that's code for a new job).

When I inevitably reach this point at a job (and it is fait accompli), I always reflect on one of the scenes in the introduction to the old *Kung Fu* TV series.  The blind Kung Fu master is training a young student of Kung Fu.  The master explains to the pupil that it will be time for the pupil to leave once he can swipe the pebbles from the master's hand. How hard can it be to swipe some pebbles from an old guy who cannot see?  To bridge the analogy to my evolution in jobs, I felt like I was grabbing a pebble every couple of weeks and by the end of a year or two, I had accumulated a lot of pebbles. I knew it was time for me to leave.

With that as a backdrop, I was extremely receptive to the opportunity at SBCL as I was exhibiting all the signs associated with job ADHD. On top of that, I rationalized that there was nothing better than an opportunity to build a business with the backing of a stable big business behind it. Their ability to finance this business eliminated a lot of the typical start-up risk. I didn't have to raise any money; the company would pay for it. How could this possibly go wrong?

During the interview process for the position at SBCL, I had the opportunity to meet with a number of people who were involved in the POC project. With a strong leaning towards wanting this to work, I did not do as thorough a job on diligence as I should have. And I did not pay as much attention to signs that the opportunity was not as great as I wanted it to be. There were clear signals that the opportunity could be more challenging than it first appeared. My soon-to-be boss (who reported to Don) was someone who seemed to be a bit out of the loop on information related to the project and I got the sense from others that she had already been marginalized.

It was also clear that there were two power positions for this project—one of which was my former colleague and mentor, Don, and the other a complete unknown and former GM of one of the regional labs. There was a lot of tension—bordering on hostility—between these two parties. That said, I did not let these warning signs dissuade me from a job that I wanted to believe would be a great opportunity. Once I started down the path to this job, there was really no turning back. I rationalized that I would be able to smooth over some of these rough areas, and probably ignored a few other warning signals. This is what some may call viewing things through rose-colored glasses...really deep rose-colored glasses. I decided to make the move.

When I announced to the folks at J&J that I planned to leave to pursue another opportunity, they were kind enough to ask if there was something that they could do to make me stay. I told them that it really had little to do with me wanting to leave J&J, and everything to do with my desire to build and run my own business. I felt like this was an opportunity I could not pass up. For the most part, my J&J colleagues were happy for me and wished me well. There were some who wanted to make sure that I realized that if I left, there is absolutely no coming back to J&J. I guess that was an attempt at encouraging me to stay by increasing the fear of leaving. I was not afraid of the future, nor was I thinking that I would ever be going back to J&J. Shows just how well I can predict the future!

The first day of my new job at SBCL was quite eventful. The R&D project managers who had been running this project for the last year organized a huge meeting with all of the key stakeholders and the two lead consultants on the project. The consultants had been tasked with developing the business plan for the point-of-care business opportunity and they were presenting the culmination of their work on my first day on the job! What great timing! I felt like I could learn everything I needed to know on my first day on the job.

The presentation was extremely detailed and had lots of slides and charts talking about how big the market opportunity was. There were also specific details about the device that SBCL would develop, which included cost estimates for different features of the device.

The longer the presentation went on, the more concerned I became. There was absolutely no reference to research conducted with patients, physicians, hospital administrators, or anyone else that would come in contact with the device. There were a lot of detail around the bells and whistles that would be built into the device itself. Much of the "research" the consultants had done consisted of interviews with internal R&D people. This is what we call drinking the Kool-Aid; we thought we were awesome... as far as we knew.

I held my tongue at the meeting for as long as I could—which in truth was not very long. I had to ask a few critical questions:

✓ Who was going to use this device?
✓ Who was going to pay for this device?
✓ What is the current alternative practice (and price) for testing?

To say that the consultants were annoyed at my questions would be a vast understatement. They were even more annoyed when I persisted with follow-up questions to their lame responses to the questions. After a few jabs each way, one of the consultants finally asked who I was and what was my relationship to this project. I informed him that I was the person who was going to be commercializing this opportunity and as a result, I needed to know a few things that did not seem to be in included in the voluminous presentation materials that the consultants had prepared. There was a collective groan from the consultants.

There were lots of charts and graphs and grand statements and platitudes, as you would expect from high-priced consultants. There was not, however, a clear understanding of the market place. Who was the customer? Who was paying for the device? What was the lowest cost alternative to the new approach? Who is most threatened by this new device? Competitors, as well as people in hospitals who could be adversely impacted by wide-scale adoption of the device? There were many, many stones left unturned.

So I got off to a flying start in my new gig! I was still excited about the opportunity and was convinced that I could "right the ship." After a few weeks of additional research and learning on my part, I determined that there was a good potential path forward. It only required one very important shift in our plans. Instead of taking 3 years and $70M to build a manufacturing facility from scratch, I recommended that we partner with one of the existing manufacturers. We would benefit from the manufacturing expertise of our partner and would be free to invest the $70M originally planned for construction of the manufacturing plant to develop the market for the device immediately. Naturally, I thought this idea was brilliant—but then I thought all of my ideas were. Not all of them turn out to be brilliant ideas, but did I mention the importance of confidence in innovation? If you don't believe, who will?

There was a surprisingly deep resistance to my suggested approach. One of the key R&D players on the team really wanted to go through the experience of literally building this business from the ground up, so he was not in favor of a partnership that would deny him that experience. A partnership would have marginalized his role on the team, whereas building a manufacturing site would create enormous job security. He was putting his personal interests ahead of the business needs.

R&D loved the plan that the consultants had put forth as it allowed them to design and build a plant from scratch. The plan meant job security for most of the R&D organization for years to come. What was troubling me, though, was that there was far more certainty over the costs associated with building the plant than there was on the potential for and timing of generating revenues. I tried in vain to get anyone to focus on a more cost-effective and expeditious path to launch. Nobody seemed to care. After getting nowhere fast with the R&D team, I began to question whether there was anyone in R&D who really understood the value of money. I also realized that I needed to elevate the discussion to the President of the Labs business. Surely, he would embrace the opportunity to save time and money and get to market as soon as possible.

The President spent a good part of his career in R&D at the labs. It seems R&D had a reputation for afflicting employees with "cash amnesia." Part of the reason this condition is more common in R&D is that money spent there is generally viewed as an investment in the future whereas money spent in almost any other department is categorized as an expense. This helps explain why the President supported a plan where cash consumption was significantly greater than the cash supply. In R&D circles that was acceptable as an investment. To me, it just did not add up...unless we were to partner with someone.

I pleaded passionately with him to consider partnering with a manufacturer in order to get us to market faster and to spend our money more wisely. Unfortunately, the President had his own idea about what sort of opportunity was in front of us. His response to my partnership approach was an unequivocal, "No." He told me that he did not want to share the "pie" with anyone else. I tried to help him understand that without a manufacturing partner, there was no "pie." He was steadfast in his resolve.

It was at this point that I determined that I had gotten into a situation that I did not believe I could fix. I have to tell you that this was the first time I had ever reached a point where I believed that the best solution was for me to stop fighting a battle whose outcome had already been determined. I am usually up for the challenge of a good fight. As upbeat and optimistic as I am about fixing just about anything, I did not have the same resolve in this case.

What was different about this opportunity? Why was I not fighting as hard and long as I had always done for what I believe? After much soul-searching, I finally figured it out. The problem was that this was someone else's passion, not mine. I airdropped into the opportunity but had no real skin in the game. I was excited about the idea of starting a new business, but not necessarily the idea of starting a point-of-care testing device business. There were many people who had spent years working on this opportunity prior to my arrival. They had the passion and fortitude to fight as long as it took for them to get what they wanted. I simply did not have it.

Fortunately for me, I maintained good contact with some of my friends and colleagues at J&J. As soon as they heard that I was not totally enamored with the opportunity at SBCL, they asked if I would be interested in returning to J&J. This was a tough one for me. I had left with absolutely no intention of returning. I loved the company and the people at the company, but it felt to me like I would be returning as a failure. I left J&J originally with a mission to start a point-of-care testing business. I had nothing to show for my efforts and now was returning to J&J…beaten.

I got over the ego side of the equation pretty quickly when I learned that the job I would return to would be a Product Director position in our international group. It was a great combination of responsibilities that I was passionate about. The role required me to help start OTC businesses around the globe. I loved the business-building aspect of the role and had always had an interest in different cultures, geography, and travel. This seemed like the perfect fit. So, a mere 9 months after I left J&J, I was back…and with a promotion to boot! So I had that going for me…which was nice! Who says you can never go back?

**Lessons learned from *Look Before You Leap!***

⊙ **Look before you leap, and keep looking after you leap!**
Question everything before, during and after you get involved
in a new venture.

⊙ **Passion is the single biggest driver of successful
innovations.** Don't air drop into someone else's passion, find
your own. Your passion is what helps you overcome the
inevitable obstacles that arise. If you don't have it, innovation is
difficult to drive.

⊙ **Beware of R&D-driven organizations.** Make sure that there
is a balance of commercial expertise alongside of the R&D
effort. All R&D and no commercialization is a recipe for failure.

⊙ **Trust your instincts.** I could have accepted many of the
conclusions of the consultants and team members I joined at
SBCL since they had more time on the opportunity. My gut
told me otherwise. Trust your gut.

⊙ **Share the pie.** Don't get greedy. The potential upside for
POC testing was huge and there was plenty of upside to share.
We should have embraced the opportunity to "de-risk" our
development and to share the upside with the right partner.

⊙ **Know when to fold them.** Sometimes you need to put all
ego aside and admit you made a mistake...and learn from it.

⊙ **Don't burn any bridges.** I did not intend to return to J&J.
Because I left on good terms, I had the opportunity to return.

# 16 | Nothing Personal... Or is Everything Personal?

This story is about two individuals who almost let their personal dislike for one another prevent them from creating a successful new business venture. The key lesson here is that you have to find a way to work through the personalities involved in business opportunities. Although it may take some time, if you are committed to finding a solution, you will eventually find some common ground even when the two parties have a personal dispassion for one another.

Recall that I was told when I left J&J that there was no coming back. At the time, I figured this was some sort of threat that they thought would force me to reconsider my decision to leave. The threat did not work, and as it turned out, I guess that the statement was really more like a loose guideline than a hard and fast rule. I had returned to J&J after unsuccessfully attempting to start a point-of-care testing business at SmithKline Beecham Clinical Laboratories. I was thrilled with the potential opportunity at J&J as I was charged with helping establish international joint ventures between J&J Consumer and Janssen Pharmaceuticals in order to extend the TYLENOL franchise around the globe. My initial targets were in South Korea and South Africa. In each of those markets, I had success launching a number of TYLENOL and other over-the-counter products. I then started to work with the South American markets. Every market had its unique idiosyncrasies, but nothing compared to my Argentinean experience.

The opportunity in Argentina was clear: bring the best

attributes of two different J&J divisions together to build the OTC business. Janssen Pharmaceuticals had a number of products that it could contribute to the joint venture, but lacked an understanding of consumer marketing. J&J Consumer Products had the consumer marketing knowledge and people who could help drive this business forward but lacked the actual products. It sounded like a very simple and straightforward opportunity to leverage the respective strengths of two sister organizations to build a new business.

On the face of it, negotiating with a sister company seems like it should be pretty simple since the two companies are part of the same parent company and should therefore be motivated to help each other succeed. But a funny thing happened when we tried to negotiate a joint venture between these two companies. The fact that they both were part of the same parent organization led them down a different and unexpected path. Each side felt that it deserved something better than they could get from an external partnership since they were on the same team. They believed that the closeness of the two companies entitled them to some tangible "extra" value.

It was far easier to negotiate joint ventures with external companies than it was with these two internal parties who believe that they were "owed" something more than they could reasonably get from an external partnership. Since both sides operated from this principal, there was essentially no common ground for mutual interests—other than the shared belief that they should be able to get a better deal. It was more challenging and took longer to negotiate a partnership because there were no overlapping interests (see figure below).

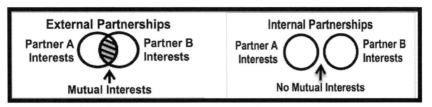

The characters involved in Argentina helped to make this partnership even more challenging. The respective Managing Directors in Argentina for the Janssen and J&J Consumer divisions hated each other. I don't use that term loosely or for dramatic effect. In fact, it is probably fair to say that I am downplaying the animosity between the two main characters who were striving to negotiate this deal. There was genuine, passionate distrust, and hatred that permeated the relationship. The only time they were ever civil to one another was when they were forced to get together to discuss the progress of the joint venture on my visits to the market. When I was with them in their country, they talked and seemed almost pleasant and friendly to one another. Once I would leave the country, all communications would abruptly stop until the next time I returned to the market. It was especially strange to me because they both seemed to be very good people. They just despised one another.

For some time, it seemed like we would not be able to bridge the gaps in order to finalize the terms of the joint venture. There was so much distrust between the two, it was just too much for the Janssen Managing Director (MD) to accept. From his view, he was providing all of the brands that would generate revenue and handing that over to unknown J&J Consumer people who would happily take full credit for success.

After considering dozens and dozens of alternatives, one solution emerged as somewhat plausible and overtime elevated itself to the status of "it's our only shot." It was clear that the MD from Janssen would not trust anyone from the J&J Consumer business to manage the brands that he would be contributing to the partnership as part of the deal. If I could insert someone whom he trusted into a leadership position within the joint venture, then he might buy into the deal. I still needed to get the MD from J&J Consumer to buy into the choice for the job, but I felt it was more important for the deal that the Janssen MD had a person he trusted leading the effort. We found the right guy who had worked at Janssen and made it happen after many, many, many months and many, many, many trips to Argentina. It took a long time because the phones apparently did not work in Argentina until I was actually in the country! (Detecting any hint of sarcasm there? Remember, they only talked when I was in the country!) I was just a big old facilitator and peacemaker.

Despite the long delays and the significant distrust that existed between the two leaders, the joint venture was launched and had a very successful and sustained period of growth that benefited both businesses. It is still one of the more successful international joint ventures we established despite the initial personality obstacles. The most amazing part of this journey was that there was never any doubt from either party that the joint venture would be a success. There was not a lot of discussion about what would happen if things did not work out. Almost the entire reason for such a painful path to partnership was "who gets credit for success?" Both managing directors wanted to get their share of the success while blocking their "partners" share in that success. I thought that these were strange times in a strange world, but have since come to realize that these behaviors are not that uncommon in corporations. Personalities are sometimes hard to overcome.

$$\odot \odot \odot$$

### Lessons learned from *Nothing Personal… Or is Everything Personal?*

⊙ **It is harder to negotiate internal joint ventures versus external joint ventures.** When both parties expect the other side to give them a better than reasonable deal (the family discount), it is hard to find common ground.

⊙ **You must understand the culture and the people in order to bridge the gaps.** Argentina is a country where negotiation is a part of life. They seem to enjoy it as a sport or a past time.

⊙ **Be creative (and relentless) in driving the solutions.** There is always a way to bring people to agreement. Even when it seems like there is no common ground, you need to continue to push to find the critical motivators of behavior. Once I understood that "trust" was the missing link, I focused my solution on a foundation that would provide mutual trust to both parties.

⊙ **Breakthroughs will always occur if you don't accept failure as an option.** There were many times when I felt like giving up on Argentina and focusing on other markets where the challenges from the top were not nearly as bad. I guess there was a little ego involved on my end as well. In a bizarre revelation, my ego would not let me accept that their egos could stop us from building a successful joint venture in Argentina. That is a lot of ego going around!

⊙ **Sometimes business is personal.** From my earliest days in business I was told that you have to learn to separate the business side from the personal side. My experience in Argentina showed me that for these two Managing Directors, the business was personal! They would rather not have a business than allow their counterpart to share in any part of a success.

⊙ **It's about the people.** The people need to know each other and respect each other in order to make a partnership work. If they do not, then find someone who both parties do like and/or respect even if it is not each other.

# 17 | Sometimes Words Have No Meaning... A Lesson in International Culture

Every market has its own unique characteristics. As we tried to establish a global TYLENOL franchise based largely on the approach that had worked in the United States, we had to recognize unique characteristics of the local market that necessitated a different approach. South Africa was no exception. We learned a lot from this developing market that was then applied back to the developed markets.

South Africa was one of the strongest economies in Africa and thus a priority market for the expansion of J&J's global OTC business. I had the opportunity to help develop OTC joint ventures by launching TYLENOL and TYLENOL line extensions. On one of my many trips to South Africa, I was enjoying one of the fine indigenous beers while at a local bar. As the Managing Director of the joint venture settled in a chair at the bar, he placed a giant brick-like item up on the bar before he ordered us a couple of drinks. I thought maybe it was a souvenir from a house construction project he had underway. I asked him what that "thing" was. He told me it was his cell phone. I was in utter disbelief. First of all, the "thing" was huge! Secondly, why on Earth would anyone carry a phone with them everywhere they went? That concept seemed completely bizarre to me. Keep in mind that this was the mid-90s and the widespread adoption of cell phones globally and certainly in the US had not yet taken off. He explained that the infrastructure (land lines) in South Africa was so bad and unreliable that cell phones were a better option for all. Wow! Here I was in a developing market and the technology in this country basically leap-frogged over the technology in developed markets. This was a classic lesson: South Africa was not burdened by the legacy of the past, so it did not have to stay with the old, traditional approaches. Rather than invest the time and expense to build a world-class communication infrastructure using traditional land lines common in the developed world, South Africa just skipped to a better technology—mobile phones and wireless communication systems. They focused on what it should be and made it so. The lesson for innovators is that you should focus on blazing your own path to the future rather than following on the path that others have taken.

Now, back to the story... we were preparing to launch TYLENOL PM (for pain and sleeplessness—but mostly for sleeplessness) in the wireless-friendly oasis of South Africa in a similar fashion to our successful launch in the U.S. Since I was the marketing "expert" from the U.S., it was up to me to share launch best practices with the South African team. This would help ensure a consistent "look and feel" to the brands. During the research leading up to the launch we discovered a really critical learning. Consumers in South Africa had no idea what "PM" meant. For many, they associated it with "post-menstrual." One small, but very important point I feel compelled to share with you: South Africa was not the United States. A typical global brand approach would be to launch PM anyway since it gives consistency across the globe. Local market be damned! But the phrase PM literally meant nothing to the South African consumer.

So, we decided to "stray" from the traditional PM name and go in another direction. To my earlier analogy regarding landlines vs. wireless, using the "PM" would have been akin to building landlines in South Africa—a huge expense that would not make any sense. We decided to go "wireless" and develop a name that leap-frogged the brand ahead in South Africa. The name that tested superbly in South Africa was TYLENOL Nightpain. This would, of course, require approval from the J&J home office in order to do so. I had painstakingly gotten all of my ducks in a row in preparation for the battle that I thought would ensue. The research and the voluminous presentation deck that I prepared all pointed in the direction of "Nightpain" being the answer.

When I presented the case to our US counterparts, who were really the "overlords" of the brand, I was expecting the worst. I knew they would fight passionately for consistency in the brand name. After all, how can you have a global brand with different names around the globe? I was prepared for a huge battle but was pleasantly surprised by the reaction I got. The head of the TYLENOL franchise said, "Wow, that's a really great name. I wish we would have launched it in the U.S. with that name." Luck favors the prepared, I guess. I did not need to cover much of the presentation I had prepared, but that was OK. They liked what we were planning to do. It was all systems go for the launch.

My counterparts in South Africa were thrilled that we could proceed with our launch. I flew the 15½-hour direct flight from New York to Johannesburg (affectionately known as Jo'burg) and enjoyed a fantastic launch meeting at a conservatory (with a massive telescope to see the stars). It was an awesome meeting and I enjoyed having the opportunity to get to know the South African launch team and to provide the keynote at the launch event. I must admit that it felt a bit odd to be touted as the global expert on the brand; especially since I probably learned more from them than they did from me. I got over it, though.

After the launch night, we had an excursion to one of the many beautiful game parks in South Africa. The countryside in South Africa is absolutely stunning. We flew from Jo'Burg across the escarpments to the Bongani Mountain Lodge and Game Park. It was a long trip to the park, but an even longer trip to get from the entrance of the park to the lodge where we were going to stay. The only way to get there was on massive Land Rovers moving slowly over rough terrain. It was incredibly scenic as we saw scores of elephant, giraffe and water buffalo. It was a very long, slow and BUMPY ride up the mountainside.

We finally arrived at the lodge area—which consisted of a number of different huts enclosed by a high wall that was intended to keep out some of the more dangerous game—lions and leopards. Did I mention that there were men all around the camp with rifles? They were there for our protection, naturally, but it was a bit disturbing nonetheless. Where was my rifle? The hut I stayed in was the same one Nelson Mandela stays in when he goes to Bongani. It was huge and had a porch off of the back that overlooked the plains hundreds of feet below. We were basically on the side of a cliff. It was a spectacular view and remains one of my fondest memories of my South Africa trips.

The first night was a little restless. I heard the sound of what was later determined to be a lion finding some game near the wall just outside of the compound. OK, I was feeling pretty secure at that point and was really excited about going out on safari to see what game we could spot…unarmed! We left in an open air Land Rover that had one of the more interesting hood ornaments I can ever remember seeing. The hood ornament was a man with a huge rifle. It was a real man and a real rifle and he was there in case any of the game in the park decided to get friendly with us. Again, I was very glad to have the protection, but it also made me wonder how safe the excursion really was. As it turned out, we saw some really cool things: a massive heard of water buffalo, two rhinoceros, a few elephant, a couple of lions, and dozens and dozens of zebras (easily the most common animal in the park).

It was a fun trip… but all good things must come to an end. I had to leave a bit earlier than the rest of the crew, so I made my way down from the cliff-top in the Land Rover and went to the local airport. I have to ask you, the reader, what you would picture as a "local" airport in a remote area of South Africa. Let me help you with this picture. The airport was more or less an indoor/outdoor airport. There was a small office area where you could check-in and there were a few people who were hanging out waiting for their flights. The airport runway was very small and mostly grass. The airport seemed to have an innovative solution to cutting the grass. They had a bunch of goats control the grass. When the planes needed to land or take off, some airport personnel then needed to "control" the goats by herding them off of the runway. When my plane arrived, I was surprised that it was a four-seater—OK, maybe a five-seater as the pilot actually had a seat as well. I admit that I was a little anxious about the flight, but it turned out to be a spectacular trip. Flying over the Great Escarpment in a small plane was quite a treat. It felt like I was flying over the Grand Canyon. The scenery was absolutely stunning.

South Africa offered me the opportunity to experience a unique culture and fabulous countryside and gave me additional learning for the world of innovation. The beauty of the setting for the launch meeting was a harbinger for the success of the South African business. TYLENOL Nightpain was the first in a series of successful product launches that created a very successful OTC business in South Africa. We definitely learned that you have to tailor your launch strategy to the specific market rather than blindly adhering to the recipe that was developed from the home market. Expensive television advertising, which was the norm in developed markets, simply would not work in South Africa as we could not afford it. Instead, we did a lot more outdoor advertising and in-store promotions in and around the biggest cities. We had to do things with more of an eye to cost-effective results. We paid attention to the unique characteristics of the market and tailored our launch plan appropriately.

The other key takeaway is that you can take a weakness and turn it into strength. In the case of South Africa, the business did not have the "luxury" of having an established professional and consumer sales force, so we started with a clean slate. We only did things that allowed us to progress quickly in this market. We did not have the burden of justifying the existence of expensive sales representatives because we did not have them. Many companies will start with the infrastructure they have in place (similar to the earlier reference to the wireless vs. land lines). If they have already made investments in the "infrastructure" they feel the need to continue to justify the existence of that infrastructure. In some cases, this leads to programs that are designed to make the infrastructure more valuable rather than to achieve the real goal of driving customer behavior as effectively as possible.

A number of pharmaceutical clients I have worked with over the years claim that they want innovative approaches for sales and marketing. When I probed further, it turned out that they were really just trying to optimize sales force productivity by giving them more stuff to do. They often asked the question, "Since we already have a sales force, how do we make them more valuable to physicians?" Again, what they should be focusing on is how to provide more value to physicians in the market (this may or may not include a sales representative), not on making the representatives that exist more valuable. The representatives' role may or may not be important to physicians in the future, but it seems always to be important to pharmaceutical companies who have already invested heavily in these "land lines." All of this wonderful learning came from a series of trips to an incredibly beautiful country that was not burdened by the U.S. infrastructure!

⊙ ⊙ ⊙

### Lessons learned from *Sometimes Words Have No Meaning... A Lesson in International Culture*

⊙ **Even when you think you have all of the answers, you can learn a lot from your students.** In this case, I represented the "teacher" from the corporate office, and South Africa was the "student" providing valuable lessons to me.

⊙ **One size does not fit all.** You need to focus on the needs of your customers, not the needs of your brand.   Conventional branding wisdom would suggest we launch TYLENOL PM—but PM had no meaning in South Africa.  We developed a brand that was more meaningful and descriptive to the local market. As it turned out, it was a better brand name than the original!

⊙ **The developing world can teach the developed world a lot.** Who would have thought that people everywhere would be walking around with their phones on their person?  Not many people would have seen that coming in 1995.  I saw it first in South Africa.  (I wish I had the foresight to invest in some wireless providers!)  Since South Africa was not burdened by a well-functioning communications infrastructure, they could leapfrog to a better solution—wireless.  Many companies are not "burdened" with significant infrastructure, so they are similarly free to "leap-frog" to a better way to influence the market.

# 18 | The Power of Observation

This story is a fun lesson about the importance of observing your surroundings and applying observations from one area to a completely new area. A common source of innovation is the application of an insight or technology from one environment to a completely different environment. In this instance, I had the opportunity to solve a very real family problem that I was facing on a Sunday afternoon many, many years ago. I had to find a new baby pacifier quickly in order to preserve the ever-depleting level of sanity that my wife and I had. The solution to this problem proved to be a pretty darned good solution to another problem that I had with the business I was running. The key for me was to apply the learning from one situation to the other. Let's take a look....

After a successful few years of building OTC businesses around the globe for J&J, it was time for me to come back to the domestic business at McNeil (J&J's OTC business). The decision to move back into a more traditional domestic brand rather than continue to build small businesses overseas was a tough one from a professional standpoint but an easy one from a personal perspective. My wife and I decided that it was time to settle down and start a family. This would not have been easy to do if I had continued my global travel month after month. Our first child provided me with a great insight that would serve as the foundation for an innovation on the business I was running at J&J.

This "classic" story from my personal innovation archives happened to me when I was 34-years-old and my first daughter, Mia, was just a few months old. My wife and I were having a grand old time attending a barbeque at a friend's house that was 25 minutes away from our home. After having a nice afternoon with friends and keeping our little bundle of joy entertained, fed and changed (not necessarily in that order), it was time to head home. The day was apparently a bit longer and a lot more upsetting to our little girl than we had suspected. She started getting a tad fussy...and then a bit cranky...and then downright inconsolable as we prepared to leave. I thought I knew just what to do to calm her down. This was a job for the old reliable binky, aka, the pacifier.

And it was at that moment, with a bit of panic I hasten to add, that we realized that "I" had forgotten a very important travel item...the aforementioned binky. For those of you that have never experienced this blissful period of a child's life, it's amazing how "brand loyal" infants can become to something as seemingly innocuous as a binky. In any event, my wife and I thought, "Hey, it's only 25 minutes...how bad could the car ride be?" Famous last words!

Mia's crying was loud, long, and became too excruciating for us to endure. As responsible parents (with fully functioning ears), it was just too much to ignore. We had to do something and it could not wait until we got home. So, on the way home, I pulled into a CVS drugstore, and then I felt like things turned into a cartoon-like setting. I was the main cartoonish character by the way. I literally ran into the store, and looked frantically around for someone who might be able to help me find what I needed. I saw someone. I sprinted, planted my feet and then skidded sideways a bit before coming to a halt just in front of the storekeeper. "Where is the baby aisle," I blurted out breathlessly. With a confused (maybe stupefied) look on his face, he pointed over my shoulder and said, "It is right behind you, sir!" He wasn't sure whether I was "messing" with him or I was just an idiot. I assure you, I was an idiot. I bolted quickly down the aisle and again came to a sideways skidding halt in front of the binky section. When I say that this section was big beyond belief, I mean it. There were dozens and dozens of different sizes, shapes, and colored binkies How could something so simple, be so difficult to figure out? Which one was the right one? If I picked wrong there would be hell to pay. Did I mention how babies develop an early affinity for the shape and feel of their binky "brand?"

And then, I saw it...out of the corner of my eye (strange expression as there are no corners in eyes if you think about it). I saw a little visual moniker. Like a beacon in the sky, it captured my attention. "Stage 1," is all it said and that's all it needed to say. My girl was less than 6-months-old, this must be the right one for her...Stage 1! That's it! Suddenly, all of the madness from the wall of pacifiers (which I nicknamed, "The Great Wall of Binky") started to make sense. There was an order, there was a rhyme and a reason. One brand was kind enough to use a beacon to reach out and speak directly to me about the brand I needed. Everything made sense in the world! I purchased my Stage 1 binky and gave it to Mia. She took to it nicely, the crying stopped, our stress evaporated and we had a very pleasant journey the rest of the way home. And that was the end of the story. Or was it?

As I reflected on how easy things had been made for me in a very complex retail setting, I could not help but think about the Children's TYLENOL business that I ran. We had a full line of products: Infant's Drops, Liquids, Chewables, and Jr. Strength Tablets. In addition, the shelf was crowded with numerous competitor and generic brands. The wall of products in children's analgesics was even more menacing to navigate than "The Great Wall of Binky." I thought to myself: "How can I make it easy for mom's to figure out what product makes sense for them?" And then it hit me. We need a beacon! And the beacon was the "Stages" concept! Why don't we apply the same concept of stages to the entire line of Children's TYLENOL products?

- Stage 1: Children's TYLENOL Infants Drops
- Stage 2: Children's TYLENOL Liquid (when kids can drink liquids)
- Stage 3: Children's TYLENOL Chewable (when kids can chew tablets)
- Stage 4: Children's TYLENOL Jr. Strength (when kids can swallow pills)

It all happened so easily, right? Good idea. People got it. Boom! It happened, right? Not so fast... this packaging change had to overcome some serious obstacles before the stages concept received its final approval for launch.

There was incredible inertia to do nothing with the Children's TYLENOL package. In fact, prior to our concept, numerous revisions to the package had been proposed, tested, and denied for years. It was a cycle that repeated itself every two to three years. There was an enormous amount of research done on different packaging. At the end of the day, however, the result was always the same. People wanted to maintain the equity in the old package—despite the fact that it looked as generic as you could possibly make it.

One other interesting point of note: part of the reason that people had assumed the package could not be changed was the image that appeared on the Children's TYLENOL package was a sketch of J&J Consumer Group's Company Chairman when he was a boy. Everyone had assumed it (more accurately, "he") was untouchable. Nobody had ever asked the chairman, but they assumed he would say no to a change.

Rejection had become an organizational badge of honor. Nobody was big enough or strong enough to overcome the strength of the existing brand, and nobody had a better answer than no. Even as I shared the story of the origin of the insight, my colleagues went through a sequence of interest followed by the reluctant acceptance of the inevitable defeat. These were very smart, driven people who were conceding defeat before there was even a battle. Were they just too "war weary" from past battles to accomplish something new?

In order to overcome the incredible power of the status quo that had thwarted past attempts to change the package, people needed to believe it could be done. They needed to suspend their disbelief. There were many legitimate attempts to change the package in the past that met the same fate: rejection. This was going to be different. I convinced people to examine some of the reasons for past failures. Upon examination, it became clear that our effort offered something that none of the previous efforts did. For the first time in the history of the Children's TYLENOL franchise, all of our different forms would be represented on each package. In essence, we not only helped mothers find the right "stage" product for their child, but we provided an "advertisement" of sorts on the package to let mothers know which product is best for the child at all ages. We had a better chance of keeping moms in our franchise for the duration of their kid's childhood. This cohesive franchise approach to the different packages offered a significantly better value proposition than anything previously attempted and helped turn doubters into supporters of the initiative.

It took some time and a lot of effort, but in less than one year—which if you understand big companies you can appreciate the "speed" at which we got this done—we had designed hundreds and tested dozens of variations of new Stages packaging, and then launched the new line of products to the public. Significantly, this was the first major packaging change to the Children's TYLENOL brand in 30 years! The change helped further differentiate our product in a very crowded space, and helped keep people within the franchise as their children aged. Finally, moms could easily determine exactly which Children's TYLENOL product was right for their kids. And, moms knew that there was a Children's TYLENOL product for every age.

Having achieved our goal, it was time to reflect on the journey. Why is it that the knee jerk reaction to anything new is rejection? Is it because the more we learn, the more experiences we have, the more we realize that some things are simply not possible? When did we learn to settle for "no" and stop trying? Why do we lose the almost careless approach that children have to trying things? Remember, the lesson from Chapter 1 *Quinn the Innovator* is that you must see past the obstacles (or mess in Quinn's case) and focus on the success you want until you achieve it.

There is another really important lesson. Opportunities are all around us. Observe your surroundings and you will find opportunities every day that you can apply to your business. When you solve your own problems, chances are you are solving others' problems as well. While it is extremely important to observe, it is far more important to "apply" your observations to your business. That is the source of value creation. And don't let anything stand in your way...not even the baby picture of the Chairman of your company!

## Lessons learned from *The Power of Observation*

⊙ **Always have your radar on for new ideas.** Opportunities are all around you every day. Think about how you can apply your observations to your business… and take action.

⊙ **Force yourself to apply learning from one area to another.** Solutions to one problem can morph into solutions to other problems. The key is that you need to take action… do something.

⊙ **Thinking isn't doing…doing is doing**. I could have shared my observation from my "screaming baby" weekend with others and talked about my idea for months without ever lifting a finger to make something happen. There is no value in thinking; there is only value in doing!

⊙ **Have the courage to challenge the status quo.** There are always good reasons why things have not worked in the past; those reasons do not need to become your reasons for not trying. Many people had assumed the Chairman actually cared about his image on the package. In reality, he only cared about what was best for the business.

⊙ **Passion—and a good story—sells.** Many former resistors of packaging change initiatives became supporters because of the story and the passion behind it. The story of how easily I was able to navigate an otherwise complicated shelf-set when scanning "The Great Wall of Binky" sold the stages concept for my brand.

# 19 | You Can Do Anything You Think You Can

This story chronicles my transition from an "intra"preneur within a large company to an entrepreneur creating new value on his own. The common thread throughout my career was my desire to create new value. I loved creating things. I seized the opportunity to get out there on my own to create my future!

This is the typical story you hear about two childhood friends who have talked about starting a business for years. Most of the time the discussions were lubricated with a few beers at various parties/social gatherings. I had known Scott Snyder since high school and over the years we had bounced hundreds of new business ideas off of each other. A good idea was defined as something that would substantially change our lives from a standard of living standpoint. This is polite code for make us a ton of money! It took us a while to finally get to something concrete—16 years after graduating from high school to be exact—something that would make us some real money! It was off to the basement of my house to conceive our new business opportunity.

I was still working my day job as Product Director for Children's TYLENOL at J&J, but at night and on weekends, Scott and I advanced our plans for a new business. Scott was working as an engineer at the latest incarnation of GE, then Martin Marietta, and then Lockheed Martin. I was working at Johnson & Johnson and was in charge of the Children's TYLENOL business. While running that business in 1999, I became fully aware of a really interesting and very cool phenomenon—the internet. I was intrigued. Back then, the only thing that people did on-line was order books or CD's. Speaking of the latter, one of those companies—CD Now—was located just a few miles from my office at J&J. They were one of the few internet businesses outside of Silicon Valley to have a national reputation and had a modest success with revenues in excess of $130M. Bertelsmann eventually bought them. Their proximity and early success helped fuel the fire for what I wanted to accomplish. If they could do it, why couldn't I?

I had dabbled a bit in the internet in 1998 but failed to appreciate its full potential for changing my life. I came across an internet business just a year prior that was really interesting to me personally. When my wife and I were expecting our first child (the "star" of the previous chapter's story) we had researched kids names in preparation. I suppose "researched" is a little too clinical a term. Actually, we simply ran out of names that we could brainstorm ourselves. I thought there might be a website that could amplify our name knowledge. We did not know whether it was going to be a boy or a girl, and we wanted to identify some names that were interesting, but not overly popular. Anyway, I came across a website, called BabyCenter.com that was really cool because it listed the most popular names historically and allowed you to look at origins of names and other neat "stuff." I was surprised how much time I spent on-line checking out different names. This was definitely a sign of things to come. For boys, I circled the wagons around a few names: Jake, Max, Luke or Zach. For girls, I thought Jessica was a cool name, but I believe at the time, it was the #1 most popular name, which disqualified it from contention. I was looking for names that would be somewhat unique.

While my wife and I both felt pretty good about the name options for the boy, we had a bit of a disagreement over the girls name. My wife thought it would be really cool thing to name the baby after her maiden name, Fallon. It did pass the test for uniqueness, and it definitely would make for an interesting "origin of your name" story. That said, I could not help but think of the character on the TV weekly series *Dallas* who was named Fallon. It was a very grown up name, and the character in the show was overly made up and had questionable moral fiber. Yes, I knew it was only a show, but these associations with names actually seemed relevant and I believed that it would actually have an influence on the type of kid our child became. In some ways, I guess I thought that the child would grow into the name, which seems kind of silly now that I have that out of my head and on paper. In any event, I had a lot of work to do in order to get my wife off of the "Fallon" bandwagon. I threw every name in the book (technically a website) at her. We read the top 100 names from every list on Babycenter.com to no avail. My wife was set on the name Fallon.

Being the persistent fellow that I was, I relentlessly threw out random names to her even up to the day and hour of the birth of our first child. One of the female names I threw out was Mia. I had known someone in college with that name and she was a cute, spunky, and fun girl. My wife paused and said, "It's a good name, and if we weren't going to name her Fallon, then that's a good second choice. But we are naming her Fallon." I accepted that as a moral victory.

My wife and I were both pretty anxious to bring this little baby into the world. We thought we'd see if some of the "old wives'" tales were true about getting labor started. My wife and I went out for spicy Thai food and we came back and walked some steep hills in the area—we were doing everything we could think of to get the baby out as spicy food and walking hills, it is alleged, helps speed the process along.

It seemed to work. Maybe it was because the spicy food makes for an environment that is too hot to handle for the baby and they just want out. I'm not sure of the exact cause and effect but her water broke that night. Fortunately for us, we went to a bunch of Lamaze classes to learn all about what we could expect and what we should do leading up to the actual birth. This included specific instruction about what to do when my wife's water broke.

Unfortunately, I forget everything I learned at Lamaze class. I was a mess—jumping around saying that we had to go the hospital right away. My wife was "cool as the other side of the pillow." She seemed to have a much better grip on the situation and a greater recall of the Lamaze lessons. She called the doctor in the middle of the night, measured the time between contractions, and was instructed to go back to bed, and go to the hospital first thing in the morning. We could wait until morning based on the time between contractions.

OK, no problem. I was a little energized when I woke up from the foggy non-sleep I maintained for the rest of the early morning and decided to work off some of the pent up energy in the yard. There is nothing like some good yard work to take your mind off "stuff." I got out of bed, dressed and went out to the yard and started transplanting a number of bushes and a small tree. Can you imagine anything so ridiculous? Suddenly, I decided that it was time to transplant a tree that had been on my "to do" list for months. I suppose this was my male "nesting" kicking in.

Around 8am, my wife poked her head outside, looked at me incredulously and said, "Don't you think we should go to the hospital?" I admit that I was a bit dumbfounded. I suppose I was in some sort of "fog of denial" that was induced by the reality that I was about to become a dad! I could not wait to be a dad, but my mind was trying its best to distract me and prevent me from actually taking the appropriate next step, e.g. driving my wife to the hospital. Anita, fortunately, brought me back to reality. I regained my faculties, realized where I was and that we were going to have a baby that day. In my final remnant of my fog of denial, I left my wheelbarrow, shovel, and pick axe out in the yard as if I would be "right back" to finish transplanting the tree. Then, we zipped off to the hospital.

Within 12 hours we had our baby. Apparently some of the morning "fog" still lingered around me. The moment after our bundle of joy arrived into the world, I actually "miscalled" our daughter as a boy. I apparently mistook the umbilical cord for something else! Imagine that... there is a 50:50 chance that I could have called the babies sex before we even went to the hospital. I then have the benefit of new information in the form of an actual visual of the baby as it emerged into the world and I still called it wrong! I'm sure there is some sort of lesson in there somewhere. Maybe it is that everyone makes mistakes... or better... nobody purposely tries to make a mistake.

I managed to take that mistake in good stride and I was now ready for the next question from the doctor, "What's her name going to be?" Although I did not particularly care for the name, I knew that I could quickly move on from mistaking the baby's sex to naming the baby girl. I proudly responded, "Fallon!" And just after I uttered her name, my wife's face got all scrunched up and she said, "Doctor, can we get back to you on that one? I want to think about it a little more." I was stunned—happily so—but still stunned. The competitor in me was a little bummed to be honest. After all, I had two major opportunities to get things right (sex of the baby and the name) and I missed both of them. I was 0 for 2 as a dad. Fortunately for me, I would have many more at bats... but still, going 0-fer out of the gate is pretty lame. (Good thing I am not the competitive type! Doh!)

Despite my stumbling and bumbling on the sex and the name, I was thrilled that we now had our first daughter and her name was "Mia." Funny enough, my entire family (2 brothers and 3 sisters) knew a girl was going to bear the burden of the name "Fallon." Many of them had similar disaffection for the Fallon name, but had long ago come to grips with the perceived inevitability of it. One of my sisters tried to get a helium balloon with the words "Welcome Fallon" on it, but with so many letters in Fallon, the balloon would not stay afloat. So she came with a blank balloon and met Mia instead.

Why on Earth would I share this story with you? Well, it is yet another example of paying attention to your surroundings and your own experiences in order to identify opportunities. I was immediately drawn to the Babycenter.com business (oh yeah, I was talking about the internet!) because I could find the information (baby's names in this case) I was looking for quickly and easily. I was not sure what the revenue model was for internet businesses but I was enticed by the fact that I could spend so much time on a website that seemed to understand exactly what I was interested in knowing. I was so intrigued with Babycenter.com that I even reached out to some of the leaders of the company to learn more about what they were doing. I thought there could be an opportunity for my Children's TYLENOL business to benefit from a relationship with Babycenter.com. Additionally, it sounded exactly like the sort of business that I'd like to join personally. I was bitten by the internet bug and I thought Babycenter.com would scratch my itch.

I put together a memo to the President of McNeil recommending that J&J buy Babycenter.com. It was a perfect fit with the "Golden Egg" of J&J; the "Golden Egg" was the phrase used internally to refer to the goodwill associated with the J&J name. The goodwill was built on the foundation of the relationship between a mother and her child. What a perfect opportunity for J&J to be involved with mothers at the exact moment the relationship between mother and child starts. I reasoned that the relationship starts on-line when the mother researches baby names and other information to prepare for the birth of their child. We (J&J) needed to be a part of that critical starting point of the mother/child relationship. It was so clear in my mind.

For our President, it was not so clear. His rebuttal to me was, "Tom, we are not in the internet business." I responded by saying, "No, we are not in the internet business, but we ARE in the relationship business and this is where our relationships with mothers are going to be formed and developed in the future." He remained unconvinced. [J&J did, in fact, purchase Babycenter.com two years later. Unfortunately, it was not on my time horizon so I missed out on that part of the value creation within J&J. I suppose I was just a little ahead of my time. Come to think of it, maybe that is why I always set my watch ahead a few minutes☺.]

After the Presidential "snub," it was clear that I had to look outside J&J to learn more about the internet. Rather than cower away in the corner, I resolved that I would just have to go ahead and start my own internet business! I'll show them. This was, in fact, reminiscent of the reaction I had when people told me not to do stand-up comedy. The more people said no, the more determined I became to succeed. After all, in 1998-99, it was all anyone was talking about—at least anyone outside any of the big established "bricks and mortar" businesses. It seemed like every day brought a new story of an awesome business that would fundamentally change our world. And there I was... stuck in a multi-billion dollar behemoth continuing to approach the market the same way it had been done for decades. Even though I was planning to try something new, I still felt stuck.

I felt just like I did when I was a kid home sick with pneumonia for a week straight. During my sickness, the area was hit by a massive snowstorm that resulted in 3 straight snow days!  All of my classmates and 2 brothers and 3 sisters were home from school and having a ball playing in the snow—all day and into the night.  Me?  I was inside, looking out at all of the fun, wishing that I could get out there and enjoy it myself.  I did get better just in time for school to reopen.  Damn!  I didn't want that to happen again… this time as an adult!

So, having the benefit of such a deeply impacting childhood scar, I was not going to feel this way again.  The internet—the equivalent of a "snow day" for a kid—was happening.  And I was inside looking out at all of the fun others were having.  I decided I'm going to do something about it.  That is when my old pal Scott and I decided to get serious about developing an internet business plan.

Of course, it was very critical that I had the full support of my wife in this process.  So I waited for the perfect time to leave the comfy confines of J&J—the creature comforts of a good, secure salary and very good benefits.  Our first child—the aforementioned Mia—was less than a year old and we had our second child on the way.  What a perfect time to set forth on an uncertain path towards an unchartered future!  Somehow I rationalized to my wife that now was the perfect time to venture out on my own.  After all, we planned to have more kids later so it would only be more difficult to wait and do this later with more mouths to feed.  Huh?  Are you following what I just said?  I know it sounds crazy now, but it made a lot of sense to me at the time.  Fortunately, it also made some sense to my wife.

She really just wanted the answer to one simple and very legitimate question:  "How are you going to make money?"  This is when I had a flashback to one of my favorite scenes from *Ghostbusters*.  After Bill Murray convinced Dan Akroyd to take out a third mortgage on his home, Dan asked Bill a simple question, "How am I going to pay this back?"  Bill's response to

Dan was the same one that I gave to my wife: "I don't know... I don't know." In both cases, the answer seemed to be sufficient, especially since it was the truth. I did not know yet how we were going to generate revenues but I was convinced that I would figure it out. Nonetheless, my wife was on-board and willing to believe if I believed. This is one of the key lessons for entrepreneurs and innovators: People will look to you for permission to believe. If you don't believe, they won't believe.

I began to network my way to the internet to have "fun" with others who had already made the leap and to learn as much as I could from them. I started to develop the first of many different internet business plans with Scott. The first step in my journey was my second departure from J&J. I left to join Qwest Internet Solutions—which was a perfect step in my journey as it allowed me to immerse myself in the world of the internet even as I spent nights and weekends building out different potential business models with Scott. It was a really important step as investors needed a reason to believe that we had what it took to succeed in the internet world and my move to Qwest gave me more knowledge (and internet "street credibility"). I really enjoyed the people at Qwest and the environment where everything was new and groundbreaking. It helped me realize that I have far greater passion for creating new things than I do for running existing things. I was following my passion.

The single biggest lesson emerging from my nascent start-up experience is that you have to be flexible and adaptable. The only thing you can know for sure about your initial plans is that they are wrong. You just don't know how wrong and in what way. You need to be able to adapt to the new information that you get along the journey to success.

The first business plan Scott and I developed was a website where you could find the best local contractors for various work around the home—from plumbing and electricity to general contracting. We intended to create a market where buyers and sellers of different services could find exactly what they were looking for. We were also excited about the prospect of customers providing real-time ratings of their experience with various providers. We envisioned becoming the sought after "seal of approval" that contractors would want and customers would seek.

After many, many meetings with potential angel investors, I developed a thin layer of Teflon protecting me from the onslaught of derogatory comments from potential investors who could not believe we missed key components in our plans. Investors had no problem making their comments personal. For them, it is part of their test. They want to see how you react. My favorite line of attack went something like this: "How could a Duke graduate with a Wharton MBA miss things which are so critically important to a business?" Again, a random movie reference pops to mind. This time, the reference comes from *Animal House*. As the fraternity pledges were on the receiving end of a high velocity paddle to their rear end, Flounder would say, "Thank you sir, may I have another." That's pretty much the way I felt as I collected verbal "paddles" from potential investors. I just took their feedback and used it to make my next pitch even better.

Eventually, after taking the abuse, and applying the learning from the feedback into a new and better plan, we were getting close to the "real deal" for an internet "smart contractor" site. And then, poof, as quickly as it came, our first big opportunity was gone. I settled down to enjoy USA Today and discovered a very interesting full page, color advertisement for a ".com" that did exactly what we were planning to do. We were scarily similar in almost every aspect, except for three pesky little areas:

1. They had already raised significant capital;
2. They already had a functional website;
3. They were advertising nationally in a paper with circulation of over 1M people.

We had a plan and a lot of pent up energy behind the plan, but as tough as it was for us to admit, we had no money, no website, and no marketing platform.  Other than those significant handicaps, we were in great shape (are you picking up on the sarcasm?).  This would be the first time that I had to really incorporate one of my most critical entrepreneurial learnings into action:  "There is no such thing as bad news...just new information."  Bad news is crippling while new information is used to get you back on the path to success.

Rather than be discouraged that a company had essentially launched the business we were planning to launch, I was encouraged by the fact that something that we thought would make sense, got funded and was going to happen.  The optimist inside me said, "We do have what it takes! We were on the right track.  We just need to move faster next time."  We had to adapt to the new information we learned and pivot to another model that works.

OK, so on to the next opportunity.  This time we focused on another painful home-related problem.  When you move into a new home—as my business partner had just done—it takes a couple of days to get the core services hooked up to the home.  And, for some of the services—like cell phones—you never knew if you had the right plan as the options seemed to be endless.  The only certainty that customers had regarding their wireless plan is the certainty that they were paying for more than they needed.  We thought there was an opportunity to make it easier for people to find the best services for their home. [As an important side-note to readers who are asking, "Why would you have to change your cell phone when you move?" Cell phone number "portability" did not come into play until 2003. Up until then, the cell phone providers really controlled the users as they would force you to switch phone numbers if you wanted to change providers.]

Hence, OmniChoice was born—which was designed to make all choices simple for all of the "pipes" into your home. Whatever service you were looking for (local, long-distance, wireless, internet, cable, satellite, gas and electricity), OmniChoice would help get you to the right plan based on your preferences, profile and usage pattern. Did I mention my partner Scott was a rocket scientist? There may be a few generalizations that you can make about really, wicked smart scientist types: so smart on so many levels, but sometimes misses things that appear to be obvious and simple connections because it's just too simple to waste brainpower on. He was the prototypical "mad" scientist. Midway through the development of the OmniChoice business plan, we were looking for something that we could hang our hat on as unique, different, and capable of providing some sustaining value to our business.

Scott casually mentioned that he had a PhD in Systems Engineering and did his thesis on Decision Modeling. He wondered out loud, "Maybe I could create something that could help people get to the right service plan based on their specific needs." I looked at him with simultaneous excitement over the possibilities this "newfound" expertise could provide the business, and surprise that it had not occurred to him sooner that a decision engine could be something of value. Nevertheless, the decision engine became the centerpiece of our website and ultimately was the sustaining value for the business as we filed a number of patents to protect it. The decision engine also helped us raise the initial round of $1.2M in private financing as it gave us a sustainable point-of-difference in the market. Not bad for an afterthought.

The fund raising effort taught me a lot about the importance of relationships. One of the key private investors in the business was Walter "Buck" Buckley. I met Buck in the mid-90's when he was at Safeguard Scientifics. He and I had an immediate and interesting connection. He graduated from UNC (where he played varsity soccer) and I went to Duke (where I attempted—and failed to make—the varsity baseball team). We had a good time dueling over the relative merits of our own school and demerits of the other's school—especially when it came to basketball. For those uninitiated in college basketball, there is a serious rivalry between Duke and UNC. I stayed in touch with him over the years as he transitioned from Safeguard to Internet Capital Group. He was one of the first people I sought counsel from when I was developing the internet business plans. He later became one of the first investors and advisors to the business I was building. His support was a critical step in the process of raising the first round of financing. His national reputation was growing in the "hey day" of the internet bubble. For the brief window of the internet bubble, he was quite literally, "The man!" Fortunately for me, he was interested in investing in my business. And because he was interested in our business, others became interested in our business.

Another key relationship that helped drive my initial fundraising efforts actually started in my childhood. Hubert Schoemaker—founder of Centocor (later purchased by J&J) was a neighbor of ours when I was young. Two of my sisters had done a lot of babysitting for his kids—and he always paid really, really well! There was one occasion where my sister was supposed to babysit but apparently forgot. The Shoemakers were desperate so I stepped in and held down the fort. It went well, and they sure did pay well! While I did not do much babysitting for them after that—not sure if they were sending me a message about how it went that evening come to think of it—I did maintain a good relationship with him.

When I had graduated from Duke, I met with Hubert Shoemaker to talk to him about possibilities of joining his business, Centocor. It was a small biotechnology business made up of mostly scientific types, so the time was not ideal for a sales and marketing type like me. There was no obvious opportunity in his business at that time, but we did stay in touch over the years.

When I put together my business plan for OmniChoice, I again reached out to Hubert Shoemaker. While he did not ultimately invest in my business, he did introduce me to his brother, Paul. Paul was a PhD professor at Wharton who had made quite a reputation in the Decision Sciences space—mostly around scenario planning. Paul was very interested in OmniChoice and seemed like he would be a strong foundational investor.

I also reached out to my brother Larry and brother-in law Ritson. The former introduced me to some people who eventually became investors and the latter became an investor himself. My network played a big role in providing us with the initial financial footing necessary to launch the business. It was really the first time I tapped into my network for direct investment in a business venture. It was a little unnerving.

The interesting thing about getting commitments from investors is that NOBODY wants to be first to sign. And NOBODY wants to be last to sign. Everybody was looking for a leading indicator that they were about to make a wise investment, so they looked to the others who were going to join the investment consortium as a source of their confidence. In this case, I had Buck committed to invest, and he was comfortable from the start, but wanted to make sure that I was able to raise enough initial capital to get the business off the ground. All of the potential partners were in and were pretty committed to making the investment as long as Buck was in. Buck was the critical first domino that would trigger their commitment.

One of the potential investors was also looking for that leading signal that Buck's investment would make, but his interest in investing shifted a number of times. He would reference conversations that he had with his colleagues that raised new concerns. The questions were always good and I did my best to address all of the questions and concerns. At some point, however, I had to push him for a decision. I worked with him patiently to try to clear each new hurdle that stood in the way of his investment.

After weeks of going back and forth, we seemed to be exactly where we were at the start of our discussion. I talked it over with the other investors and got their support for proceeding with the fundraising without this potential investor's support. I called the investor to let him know that while we appreciated his interest in OmniChoice, we were going to close our round of financing without him. Within 24 hours, he had signed the necessary papers and joined the other investors to complete our initial financing of the business.

The fundraising experience taught me an important lesson. If you seem desperate for investment, you are. If you seem confident enough in your plans for the business that you don't need additional investment, people are more willing to invest. In other words, the less money you need, the more people are willing to invest.

Once we established our initial web presence, I was in a position to do what every CEO must do…raise more money. It is a never-ending cycle. I had met with so many venture capitalists, wealthy individuals, and potentially interested "strategic partners" that my head was spinning. One of the more interesting potential strategic partners was Exelon Capital Partners. I connected with their CFO who was intrigued by the business model. We began more serious discussions with them in January. It was not long before we were exchanging term sheets with Exelon. We had settled on an investment of $15M for a post-money valuation of $45M. Just a bizarre aside, Google was valued at $25M at this time. On paper, we were more valuable than Google! Unfortunately, paper did not count for much. OmniChoice was not able to sustain the same trajectory that Google did. I wish it had!

While we had agreed on the post-money valuation with Exelon, the final details of the negotiations dragged on into May. This was a bit of a problem on two fronts. First, unbeknownst to anyone else at the company, we were going to run out of cash in July. Second, the first signs that the internet "bubble" was bursting came in March of 2000. The NASDAQ had reached its peak in early March and lost more than 10% of its value in 10 days. The sign of what was to come was certainly there. Was I nervous? Heck, yea!

Fortunately for me, many traditional (and sensible) metrics of success had been laid to waste during the internet bubble. Many people convinced themselves that there was an entirely different business model. This new model required a lot of cash as fuel, and would deliver exponentially greater returns to those investing in this future model. Exelon—an otherwise slow moving behemoth—was enticed by the prospect of succeeding in this new space and transforming their stodgy image. I believe it was Memorial Day of 2000 when Exelon finally signed the papers agreeing to invest $15M in the business. The papers were signed! I was relieved...sort of.

The papers were signed. The deal was done. Sounds simple, right? Another week passed by and all I could thing about was that we had less than 1 month's worth of cash on hand. I waited, and waited, and waited. Finally, I got the call from the bank that the first $10M had been transferred into our accounts. Until the money is in the bank, the money is not in the bank. We were now ready to rock! I came back to the office once the money was in the bank and played Peter Gabriel's "Big Time" over and over again at a fairly high decibel (much to the chagrin of our corporate neighbors) as it seemed like the appropriate song for the times. We were planning to make it big time!

In the span of 9 months, we had grown from my partner and me to 52 full-time employees and 20 contractors. I felt like all I did was interview people for jobs. Within a year, thanks to the treadmill of interviews and hires we were running, we had outgrown our space and moved to a much bigger location— 10,000 square feet. While we needed more space, I am quite sure we did not need this much more space. And, in retrospect, we definitely did not need the burden of the significantly greater "fixed cost" to our monthly burn rate (the pace at which a business uses—or burns—cash) that came along with the larger space in the form of rent. The bigger location had another cost. We lost a little of the vibe that made us special. I missed the closeness of the offices, cubes and lone conference room from the first office.

While I had some discomfort spending more of our cash reserves on our new "digs," our investors where still caught up in the myth of internet start-ups. Spend money now...raise more money...make money later. In a telling sign of the times, the revenue component of internet businesses lagged significantly behind the "eyeballs" that you were able to attract to your business and the "stickiness" with which you are able to keep your eyeballs coming back. Investors were more concerned about the traffic to your sight (eyeballs) and the frequency of revisits (stickiness) than any revenue targets. The belief was that the former two were necessary precedents to the latter. To continue with my earlier "snow day" analogy, investors had financial "snow days' which meant that all of the typical financial requirements could take the day (month/year) off! And back then, you never had to make those days up. "If you did not spend the money you had," the misplaced logic argued, "you cannot raise more money to increase your company's valuation." Can you imagine being pressured to spend more money so that you create the need to raise more?

I recall getting a lot of "spirited" pressure by my Exelon board members to spend money faster. We had developed a marketing plan, driven largely by key affiliate relationships that seemed to make sense. We would drive people who are looking to change their local, long distance, wireless, paging (yes that was once a service), internet, cable, satellite, electricity and gas plans to our website. Once there, they would go through our optimization engine (the OmniOptimizer), which directed them to the right plan based on their unique preferences, profile and usage patterns. Rather than unleash the marketing plan—and the $4M it took to execute it—I decided it would be prudent to test to see if, in fact, we could get customers to transact this way (keep in mind that on-line transactions for anything other than books and CDs was an alien concept).

This seems like the appropriate time to highlight a critical lesson in business. Cash is king! This is a foundational principal for a start-up business. If you have cash, you can do things. Without cash, you have no business. At the risk of simplifying a key business principal, get as much cash as you can as soon as you can and spend as little as possible as late as possible. In short, get and hold onto the money!

My board of directors wanted me to execute our plan as it was written in the Business Plan. I wanted to conserve our cash and test our model to see if our assumptions in the plan were correct. We needed to see if we could drive people to our website, get them to optimize their plans, and then connect them to those plans through our site. We did the test and successfully drove more than 1 million people to the website, and roughly 5% of them went through the optimization process. This would have been outstanding if they all transacted on-line for the service they optimized on our website. That activity would have generated a cool $7.5M for the business and put us in a great position to raise additional money and continue to grow our business.

But here was the problem. In 2000, people were more comfortable calling the companies who offer the services directly. There was still a lot of skepticism and mistrust around transacting on-line. We showed that we could get people to come to our site and optimize their plans, but we could not get them to use our site to transact on-line with a company nobody recognized. Instead, they used our service to find the right plan and then called the service provider directly on the phone to sign up for the plan. This was a great value to the consumers and the service providers but it left us with nothing to show for our efforts. We had no revenues in that world. Cool business model, except for one very important thing…it did not make us any money. Rut ro! This was important "new information."

Having successfully proven that we could not make money with our original model it was time to adapt again. We needed to shift the focus of our business to one that could make money. Remember: experiments never fail…they just provide learning. We got learning that helped us figure out where to go next. It was time to fish where the fish were. Rather than continue to invest tons of money trying to drive consumers to our website to optimize their service, we decided we would simply deliver our service where the customers already went—to the service providers directly. That was the necessary pivot for the business.

The shift we made was to sell our optimization platform—as a software solution—to the service providers. The service providers could then allow their sales and customer service agents to use our optimization platform to get customers to the right plans. The core decision model at the centerpiece of the technology could also be used to determine the optimal combination of features that customers were willing to pay for. Consumers liked having the ability to tailor their plans to their own needs, and service providers liked being able to provide services that felt more customized to meet consumer needs. It was a really cool and necessary transition for our business...but it was not without a lot of pain.

As we made the transition to a software/technology business-to-business (B2B) model, I lost some of the enthusiasm I had for where the business was headed. I loved the original challenge of influencing consumers to take certain actions. I was not as thrilled about the new challenge of convincing service providers of the merits of our technology platform for their call centers. It was the necessary shift that the business had to take, but it became a software sales business rather than the consumer marketing business I had originally envisioned. There were some interesting components to the new model, but the business model did not have the same appeal to me.

The biggest challenge for the business was that we shifted to an entirely different (B2B) selling model with a sales and marketing team designed for the original business-to-consumer (B2C) model. We underestimated how long it would take us to sell the software to the service providers. Our sales force was not built to sell the service providers. We needed to adapt quickly, but adaptation took time. The most attractive initial market was the wireless provider and we eventually had our first successful sale to Cingular Wireless, but it took more than one year from the transition to our new model to our first sale. That is a long sales cycle... too long.

In the meantime, the realities of the internet bubble bursting hit our business hard. Our Exelon investors indicated that they were not going to move forward with the final $5M installment of their investment as outlined in the signed terms of our agreement. We had done everything that we had committed to do—delivered a marketing plan and the first 5 customers (in the old model). Having witnessed and experienced the carnage of many of the other investments they had made, they simply had to do something different. While I was sympathetic to what they were going through with their portfolio companies, I was more concerned about what we were going through and how their failure to uphold their investment agreement would impact us.

After fruitless discussions with Exelon about their obligation to our business, I realized that they were not planning to change their position regarding their investment without a bit of a nudge. I produced that "nudge" by hiring a law firm to sue them for breach of contract. This did get their attention. They came back with an offer of ½ of the money they owed us in exchange for agreements to ratchet down the company and preserve it—the proverbial "lifeboat" strategy. Upon thorough review with our counsel, we felt we had a strong chance of winning this lawsuit. Exelon must have sensed the same thing as they started to plant the seeds of discourse into our business.

We eventually negotiated an agreement for a smaller amount of funding from Exelon in exchange for dropping the lawsuit and pursuing the lifeboat strategy. An important lesson here was that as unpleasant as your circumstances may be, you need to accept them and move onto productive action as quickly as possible. I knew that we did not have enough money to get us through the downturn in the internet businesses. I had put unreasonable hope on the fact that the lawsuit would yield us the money that would help us bridge to success. I failed to appreciate the dynamics within our investor's organization. As I learned years later, they had already determined that this investment would be a total loss, so their actions reflected that determination. Had I focused a little more attention on our investor's issues and needs, perhaps it would have yielded a more positive agreement.

In any case, since I can't rewrite history, I need to just tell it like it was. The combination of the change in the business model—to a software as a service model—and my feeling of abandonment by my investors left me with little zest for the business that I had put so much time and energy into building. It was time for me to leave. I did not know what I was going to do next, but I did know enough about myself to follow my passion. The prior two-year run felt more like 4 or 5 years and I was ready to do something new. One of the key learnings from OmniChoice was to focus on the intersection of:

⌘ What I love doing;
⌘ What I am good at doing.

I had enough experience (made enough mistakes) that I could be completely honest with anyone and not try to convince anyone that I am the right person for something that I would either avoid doing or that I was not particularly good at. In my younger days, it would have been tougher for me to admit this, but I was no longer young. I was experienced!

We began winding the company down—which we called "preparing it for sale." We let go all but a few of the core people required for on-going management and potential transition of the company assets. It was a difficult time, but it was definitely the right thing to do. As part of the "winding down," I resigned my position as CEO and stayed on as Chairman to see us through the ultimate sale of our business. We eventually sold the business to Call Vision who was later purchased by Verisign.  In the meantime, I had left to pursue two very different but nonetheless interesting opportunities.

### Lessons learned from *You Can Do Anything You Think You Can*

⊙ **The only certainty around your original plan is that it is wrong.** You just don't know how wrong and in what directions, until you start doing stuff!  There should be few things in your business that are "hard-coded."

⊙ **Be flexible and adaptable.** Focus on what it takes to succeed, not on what you originally planned to do. Adapt as you learn.

⊙ **Relationships matter.** This is really the "power of networking… part II."  Many of my investors were a direct outgrowth of my personal relationships that I had maintained for years.

⊙ **Don't hire and grow ahead of your demand.** Let the demand for your product or service dictate how quickly you hire personnel.

  - o Hire only those people that are critical to achieving profitability;
  - o Hire people who have demonstrated flexibility, agility and adaptability.
  - o Don't spend too much money in rent.

⊙ **The money is not in the bank until the money is in the bank.** Even when the papers were signed for the investment, I could do nothing until the money was literally in the bank.

◉**Contingent funds may never materialize, so don't expect them.** This is a corollary to "the money is not in the bank until the money is in the bank." If there are contingencies, that represents a lever for the VC to argue against fulfilling that commitment of funds. We filled our side of the commitment, but our VC decided they would not fill theirs.

◉**Cash is king.** Get it quickly. Spend it slowly. Hold onto it. It is your business's lifeline.

◉**There is no such thing as bad news...just new information.** Unexpected things will happen all the time. Bad news will cripple you and prevent you from making the appropriate adjustments to your business. Treat the same "news" as new information and you can adapt your business based on the new market reality. You are then on the path to success.

◉**You can make something from nothing.** Combine a vision with the drive and passion to achieve it and you can do almost anything.

◉**Every potential investor loves your business idea until it is time to write a check.** I don't think I had anyone say they did not like my business but I probably had 60-70 potential investors say they loved it but chose not to invest. Investment is a sign of their genuine "love" of your business.

◉**You generally know a lot more about your business than most investors or venture capitalists.** It is your passion and your business. Venture Capitalists are like business gamblers. They are playing the odds that one of their bets will win. There is a lot of luck with gamblers and Venture Capitalists. They usually don't know more than you, just different things than you do.

⊙ **Don't put blind trust in your investors.** You do not know all of the things that factor into their decision-making. There may be times when your interests are at odds with their interests.

⊙ **Trust your instincts and experience.** You know the business and you live with the decisions you make. Don't make the mistake of doing what your investors tell you if it goes against what you believe. If I had, we would have spent all of our money in the first year because my investors want me to spend money faster.

# 20 | Butt I Care!

This is a story about something that I observed in the biggest and busiest city in the United States that made a huge impression on me as to the potential impact that each individual can have in a company. More specifically, individuals who take accountability for things make a huge difference. The key is accountability! Rather than look the other way or claim to be too busy they take the time to fix something regardless of whether it is technically their responsibility. I observed someone who saw the city as his own and he was determined to do his part to make the city more like what he wanted. He did not point fingers at others who should have been doing a better job...he just decided to make a difference himself! And here is the story...

I was scurrying around New York City in the middle of the summer looking for new investors for my start-up internet business. I had recently closed our second round of funding for Omnichoice.com (details available in Chapter 19 of this book of entertaining knowledge!). In any event, it was a very hot, muggy day in the city. The cab I was in was "blazing" along at nearly 2 mph. Did I mention that it was really, really hot out? Did I also mention that the air-conditioning in the cab was not working? I do suspect that whenever you run into the old "broken" air conditioner in a cab that you suggest that they try to turn it "on" just to see if it is really broken. Sometimes it is that very simple act of turning the a/c on that miraculously "fixes" the air conditioner. A few cab companies have been known to try to save a little money on hot days in traffic by not using the perfectly working A/C in the cabs. Oh, and the manual windows only rolled down part way. Anyway…I digress. The only "breeze" that I got in the sloth-like cab was generated by the dozens of pedestrians who were walking on the sidewalk as the cab moved imperceptibly on the roadway. Yes, the pedestrians were moving faster than the cab! I thought for sure that I would be late for the meeting I had scheduled with a potential investor on the other side of the city.

So there I was watching the world pass me by (literally) from the rolled down window of my snail-like cab. I decided to pass the time (and tried to lower my rising level of stress) by doing a little people watching. I tried to figure out what people did simply by observing the way people were walking. It worked for a little while. I kept myself somewhat amused, and then something really caught my attention.

There was a fairly sophisticated looking businessperson in a business suit despite the extreme high temperature of the day. He was walking at a slightly faster, and more determined pace than most of the other pedestrians. He was doing a nice job of watching where he was walking as he had his head down to ensure that he was not surprised by any unforeseen, unwanted obstacles (there are dogs in NY!). Suddenly, he slowed his brisk pace to a stop, he then backed up a few steps, looked intently at the ground and reached down to pick at something that was in between the concrete slabs on the sidewalk. After a little prying, he rose victoriously. He had what he was looking for. I was really curious what would cause such an obviously busy man to stop and pick something up. Was it a rare coin, or something else of potential value? It must be something really interesting.

Wait a minute! As the object of his obsession became visible, I was in disbelief. The man took the object, turned and walked briskly to a nearby trashcan and threw the object into the trash.

He then resumed his brisk pace down the sidewalk to his eventual destination. Any guesses as to what object had stopped this man in his tracks, forced him to pick it up and throw it away? How about a cigarette butt! Yep, that's what it was. This very busy, very determined (and seemingly successful) businessperson had stopped to dig out a cigarette butt that had been caught in the crevice in the sidewalk.

He took it upon himself to clean up HIS city. He did not point fingers at the sanitation department or complain to the Mayor's office for failing their duties. He did not say "somebody should really pick that up." No, he took personal responsibility and accountability for the things that he COULD control. He could pick up the butt and throw it away. And he did. He wants his city to be clean so he did everything he could to make it clean. This was his city. Talk about accountability!

This is the sort of accountability that drives innovation in companies. It takes an individual who takes personal ownership of making the necessary changes. Whether the change is big or small, individuals make it happen. How often in business do you see people in similar situations when something is obviously not the way it should be (the cigarette butt) and yet they remain on the sidelines just like the hundreds or thousands of pedestrians who passed that same butt and did nothing about it? Many business people relieve themselves of their own burden of responsibility by pointing fingers at the inadequacies up and down the management ranks, conveniently insulating themselves from any personal accountability for resolving the problem. If you want a clean city, do something about it! If you want something fixed at work or at home, do something about it! It is up to you!

## Lessons learned from *Butt I Care!*

⊙ **Be accountable.  You are in charge of your environment.**
If you don't like the way things are, do something about it.
Don't complain about or point fingers at someone who did not
do their job.  Do what you can to make things the way you want
them to be.  If not you, who?  If not now, when?

⊙ **Take action...it may be contagious.**  No matter how big the
challenge, you can control what happens.  The pedestrian could
have ignored the cigarette butt, or he could have convinced
himself that this small act would make little difference on the
cleanliness of the city.  Instead, he did his part...and maybe,
just maybe inspired others to do theirs.

⊙ **Small contributions by individuals can make a huge
impact.**  Set an example of the sort of behavior you are trying
to drive.  This person had no idea that anyone was watching
him clean up the city.  But someone was!

⊙ **"Be the change you want to see."**  This is either a direct
quote or a reasonable facsimile of a quote attributed to Ghandi.
Walk your talk.

# 21 | How to Buy a House Without a Job: A Lesson in Risk Management

This story is about the role of "risk" in achieving your vision. While buying a house in the neighborhood of your dreams may not constitute an "innovation," recognizing that opportunities are fleeting and taking the necessary action to achieve your vision are the steps that drive innovation. This story speaks to the mindset of an innovator (me) who was willing to take significant risk in order to achieve his goal. Who in their right mind would put a binding bid on a house when they had no job with which to secure a mortgage? Choose one or more of the following answers:

A. A fool.
B. Someone with an "innovators" mindset who was comfortable managing risk and confident that all would work out in the end.
C. Nobody. This is a trick question.
D. A and C

The answer is actually B, although you could also make a case for D. You just have to believe that it will all work out in time. Here is the story...

It was time to move onto the next thing after my marathon sprint with OmniChoice. I used to say that running a start-up was like sprinting through a marathon! You need to move quickly, but also recognize that it is a very long race. I did not know what my next thing would be when I left OmniChoice, but I was sure that I would find something interesting. I left OmniChoice (almost two years to the date after I started it) and began exploring a number of business opportunities. Having made the transition to the internet/technology world, I was much more marketable in many different ways. There was a dearth of talent in the market with real world internet experience, and I had quite a bit, so I felt like that would be something that could be pretty valuable. I ended up interviewing for three jobs at nearly the same time. One job was head of sales and marketing for an internet agency called Intermedia. Another job was the head of IT for GlaxoSmithKline's Consumer Healthcare division. And the third job that appeared to be most likely to happen was to head up the consulting practice for one of my former investors.

Just one other important aside, at the time that I was "exploring my options," which is code for "unemployed," my wife and I saw a house in the neighborhood that we had always wanted to live in. The neighborhood was awesome—43 homes in a community around a lake (stocked with fish), man-made beach and tennis courts. There it was: the neighborhood of our dreams where our kids could grow and prosper was calling us. We looked at the house. My wife loved it, and I hated it. Mind you, I loved the property. I just hated the house. After much discussion we agreed that we would go for it! I guess that shows you who the real head of the household was…my wife. There was just one small technicality. Having no gainful employment, it would be really tough—even in those days—to get a mortgage without a job.

The house would have to wait. Or would it? I figured that there was very little likelihood of the stars aligning (right house, right neighborhood) like this again in the future once my job situation worked out. More likely, once we passed on this opportunity, I would likely find a job, but our window of opportunity to move into our dream house and neighborhood would have closed. The classic "day late and a dollar short" analogy comes to mind. I knew in my heart that I had to do something now or the opportunity would be lost. It would never be the "perfect" time because perfect never happens.

I talked with family and friends about what I should do and all of the advice and counsel was completely consistent. "There is no way that you can put a bid on this house until you have a job. There is just too much risk." They were all right...but I did have this streak in me where I don't like to listen to people when they are aligning against something that I really want to do (see Chapter 4 and Chapter 19 as a reference!). I also knew that this opportunity was fleeting and that if we waited for the "time is right" for me, the time would not be right for the house. I did what I always do. I took my chances that I would figure things out on the job front in time. I bet on me.

I put my initial bid on the house—which was a painful decision but one that I had sufficiently rationalized in my own mind. Now I am wondering whether the astute reader picked up the word "initial" in the last sentence. If you did, were you wondering whether that was intentional on my part? Uh, yes, it was quite intentional. As it turned out, there were a number of interested parties who all had put in bids on the house we wanted. If I wanted the house I was informed, I had to raise my bid significantly in order to get it. Did I mention that I was officially unemployed at the time? I still had confidence that I was going to land one of the jobs that I had been pursuing, so I upped the ante and we ended up getting the house. I put in a late closing date—June, which gave me 4 months to find a job, sell our house and get a new mortgage. Funny thing about mortgage companies...they tend to give mortgages to people who have gainful employment and have an aversion for lending to folks who are unemployed. Piece of cake! What was there to worry about? I had a four-month runway to get a job.

The one job that I thought was in the bag (the consulting gig) blew up after I put my binding bid in for the house! Rut ro!

That did not feel good. Damaged, yet undaunted, I was then left with the other two opportunities—Intermedia (an internet agency) and GlaxoSmithKline (GSK). Like I said, I started the interviews for the positions at the same time. Within 6 weeks, I was employed by Intermedia as its new head of sales and marketing working for a really cool CEO. The process at GSK continued for a total of 9 months, at which time they made me an offer that was too good to pass up. Though I really loved the type of work I was doing at Intermedia, I could not pass up the significant salary, bonus, and options package GSK gave me. In fact, the GSK job allowed me to knock down and build a new house in the neighborhood that we just moved into. Now I had the house I wanted and the neighborhood I wanted! It was all good…just as I knew (ok, maybe hoped!) it would be. You create your future by believing in it first.

## Lessons learned from *How to Buy a House Without a Job: A Lesson in Risk Management*

⊙ **Sometimes you have to take risks to achieve your goals.** If I waited for perfect, I would have missed the opportunity. I had to take action and a bit of a risk to get what I wanted.

⊙ **If you see what you want, go for it! You may never have the opportunity again!** If you wait for all of the conditions to be right for you to act, you may never act at all.

⊙ **When you give yourself no option but to succeed, you will succeed.** I had no option but to secure a job within a very short period of time. Because I had no option, I was very focused and made it happen. I think this is a corollary to the "where there is a will there is a way" theory.

# 22 | The "Top-Down" Approach Isn't Always Best

Just when GlaxoSmithKline thought they had gotten rid of me for good, like a boomerang, I was back. In this last iteration at GSK I had a number of really interesting innovation experiences that shed further light on what it takes to drive innovation in large corporations. As I may have stated earlier, people are the premium and process is the commodity especially in large corporations.

In this latest and most fascinating incarnation of me at GSK I served as the Vice President of Information Technology and Global Head of e-Marketing for GlaxoSmithkline Consumer Healthcare. What made it so "fascinating?" Well, to start with, I was not an "IT guy" and I didn't play one on TV! I had always been a sales and marketing guy who was interested in creating new value by doing things differently. The fact that someone like me, who I confess suffers from "Job Attention Deficit Disorder" proceeded to spend 6 years in an "IT" role was remarkable to me. Up until that point in my career, the longest tenure I had in any job was 2 years. There must have been something that kept me attracted to this job for me to stay as long as I did. It was the opportunity to create new value for the business from a function (IT) that had traditionally been more associated with business support versus business driver. I wanted to drive! Let me fill you in on the story…

As I alluded to in Chapter 21, after I stepped down as CEO of Omnichoice, I explored a number of different alternatives. The two most interesting were the Head of Sales and Marketing for a small internet agency, called Intermedia, and the VP of Information Technology for GlaxoSmithKline Consumer Healthcare, a large global enterprise. I started the interview process for both opportunities at the same time. I was offered and promptly accepted the job with the internet agency within 6 weeks, and was really excited about building up the business with the President and CEO—Ashesh Shah. I really enjoyed the work, energy and vibe around the business and was in no hurry to explore other job opportunities. That said, I did allow the process with GSK to continue.

The GSK "process" did not start out as a job interview as I originally had planned to sell them on consulting work. My first-ever boss, Lou Manzi, helped to arrange a meeting with the Chief Information Officer (CIO)—Ford Calhoun. I met with him and talked to him about what I thought I could do for GSK. Much of what I described as potential opportunities for GSK focused on the intersection of technology and business strategy. That was the nexus that would generate breakthrough value for GSK. Ford said that he did not see an obvious opportunity to bring me in as a consultant but he wanted me to talk to one of his direct reports who was in charge of the Global Consumer IT organization. I met with him and he also failed to see an obvious fit for consulting work, but at the end of our meeting whether I thought I could run a global IT organization. I laughed. No, literally, I laughed out loud (LOL!) and said that I never thought that "IT" and "I" would be in the same sentence together. That said, I had built and run an IT organization when I started my internet business which was chock filled with programmers, developers, architects and other folks who preferred darkness to light. I told him I absolutely could do it, but I warned him that I would focus on leveraging technology to drive sales and marketing, which was not typically what "IT types" did. Undaunted, they wanted me to interview for the position.

The "official" interview process drifted slowly and seemingly aimlessly for months. I had a few phone interviews and then a couple of face-to-face interviews, which culminated with a dinner meeting with the Global President of GSK Consumer, Jack Ziegler. I continued my straightforward approach to the opportunity. If they wanted me for who I was then it could work. If they wanted me to be somebody I was not...that would be a non-starter. I told them that I was probably the wrong person for the job as they were likely looking for someone with more direct technical expertise. I reinforced continually that my focus—should I get the job—would be to leverage technology to drive sales and marketing initiatives, which is not typically what IT people, did. While I had built and run a business loaded with IT professionals, I was truly a marketing/general manager type. This is probably not the best approach for those job seekers in the audience but it created a bit of intrigue about my candidacy. The more I told them that I was probably not what they are looking for, the more curious they became.

Because of my directness during the interviews, a few people I spoke with wanted to make sure that I understood that I was actually being interviewed for a job. I assured them that I did know, but that it was in my best interest, and the best interest of GSK, to be completely transparent about my strengths and passion. I told them that if they wanted someone who would use technology to drive sales and marketing initiatives, then I was the right guy. If they wanted someone who would be knee deep in the technology and focus on the back-office business processing side of IT, then I was not their man. I had reached a point in my career where I felt no compulsion to try and convince them that I was the right fit if I was not. If they wanted me for who I was and what I could bring to the table then that would be great. If not, then we could part friends.

As it turned out, we did not part friends as I was extended a job offer and accepted the position. I was now an "IT" guy! From the first interview until I accepted the position, the process took an astounding amount of time—9 months to be exact! Such is life in big companies. The biggest reason I took the job was because I felt that I could have a bigger impact on a bigger stage at GSK and my two new bosses agreed to give me the additional responsibility of managing global e-marketing for the consumer division.

For a number of years, I really loved what I was doing. I was the "free radical" in an organization that was very traditional and conservative. I was able to follow my passion for the new and different. I tried a lot of new things in my role and got IT involved in numerous business-building initiatives. Importantly, I became quite adept at handling the abuse of non-believers who would try to kill good, original ideas simply because they were different and "not invented here." If I had a nickel for every time someone asked me, "Why is IT involved in this?" I would have been a very wealthy man. The bottom line was that I did not really care about the organizational boundaries. I only cared about driving more value for GSK. I learned a lot of lessons in how to get things done, and how not to get things done.

I also learned that many people in the organization would go to great lengths to try to kill initiatives. People would resort to this sort of passive aggressive behavior after they unsuccessfully tried to derail the idea with their direct confrontational approach. Once they realized I would not give up on the idea that they were trying to dismiss, they thought they might have better luck simply questioning why I was the one working on delivering the idea. It was classic. And in a strange way, the resistance I generated energized me. The more resistance I got, the more I knew that I must be onto something big! Why else would people resist?

One of the first opportunities I pursued that generated significant resistance was called the Tailbrands project ("Tailbrands" was the name given to the non-promoted pharmaceutical brands at the "tail" end of their patent life). Since I oversaw the global e-marketing for the consumer division, I was well aware of the different experiments we were undertaking to try to drive our consumer business using targeted, cost-effective on-line efforts.

One of the more successful experiments was for a product called Remifemin (for women's hot flashes). The strategy was brilliant in its simplicity. I would love to tell you that it was due to some incredible insight or that we were just smarter than the competition. But I can't. The reality is that it was born out of necessity. We could not spend money we did not have, and there was no way that we could afford to spend the sort of money that J&J put behind advertising for Remifemin's leading competitor, Healthy Woman. We had to come up with a better, less expensive way to get consumers to purchase our product.

We settled on the idea of on-line sampling. It was really all that we could afford to do. We figured that women who are searching for the condition are likely to be interested in a sample of a product that can help them. After they used our sample, we believed they would buy the product. That was our hypothesis. As it turned out, we were on to something. Despite our competitor's significant investment in television and other advertising, Remifemin's sales overtook Healthy Woman's with a simple, cost-effective on-line sampling campaign. We utilized search engine optimization and targeted on-line tactics to drive the sampling initiative. In short, we spent money smarter because we had no alternative. We did not have a lot of money so we focused on what we could do with what we had—just like any entrepreneur would do. One of the things I have come to realize in business is that when you have money you tend to do stupid things. When you don't have it...you have to be smart.

The results of Remifemin's on-line sampling effort were quite strong. This initiative dramatically:

- ✔ increased market share and consumption;
- ✔ reduced the cost of acquiring customers;
- ✔ reduced the cost and time for research.

Based on this success, I designed a program that would drive similar on-line efforts in order to drive sales of some of the non-supported prescription (Rx) brands. The e-marketing theory went like this: If we could drive such a significant increase in sales for an OTC product using only on-line efforts, we should be able to drive similar results for non-supported Rx brands. It sounded like a darn good theory, but there is a big difference between consumer and prescription brands. The latter requires a doctor to write the script before a patient can have it filled at a pharmacy. That said, if success could translate to the Rx side of the business, there was much more money that the company could make. The funny thing about good theories is that they tend to attract a lot of resistance—especially when theory flies in the face of the prevailing practices and threatens the sanctity of the status quo.

I had the great opportunity to see first-hand all of the passive aggressive behaviors that people in organizations exhibit in order to kill new ideas. I call it "death by one thousand paper cuts." That is truly what it was. No single objection or blow to your effort is harmful enough to kill your idea, but the accumulation of one thousand of these tiny, pesky "paper cuts" will bleed you and your idea to death.

The initial review of the idea with my boss, Ford Calhoun was interesting. On the one hand, he was excited about the possibilities of what I was suggesting doing for non-supported Rx brands at GSK, but on the other hand, he pushed hard to increase the potential impact of my initiative. He bluntly told me that what I was suggesting did not amount to a fly on the back of an elephants butt. (Truth be told, the language he used was a little more colorful than that, but you get the message.)

He helped me understand that I could only get the support of the executive leadership team if the organizational impact was significant to the corporation. He clued me in. Tens of millions in sales or bottom line profit would be nice, but until it gets into the multiple hundred million dollars, nobody on the executive committee would be motivated to do anything other than what they were already doing. In other words, I needed to make a good case for why my initiative should become a priority for the company. Important safety tip! Thanks, Ford. This was a good lesson in perspective. To an entrepreneur like me, tens of millions seems like an awful lot of money but to a multi-billion dollar company it may not make it on the radar.

I took this to heart and considered how the learning from the Tailbrands e-marketing initiatives could be applied more broadly to the major Rx brands. That is when the financial picture got pretty interesting as the savings from focusing on targeted on-line efforts with patients could have a huge impact on the in-line brands. I refined my assumptions, became a bit bolder and made the case. The next thing I knew, I had an audience with the CEO.

The review with him went very well. I made the case for testing this e-marketing theory on a few of the non-supported pharmaceutical brands. It would be easy to see the specific impact of the internet-based solutions since there was no other promotional activity to muddy the waters on the brand we selected for our experiment. Once we learned what worked, we would then apply the learning to the major supported brands and realize a much more significant impact across the pharmaceutical business. He was genuinely engaged and seemed excited about the prospects of creating more cost-effective approaches to supporting our brands. He gave me the go-ahead I was looking for...sort of. It sounded like a "yes," but as I was getting up to leave our meeting, I was a little uneasy that things had actually gone too smoothly.

I needed to make sure that he was agreeing to what I was proposing. As I was leaving our meeting I pulled a Colombo "Just one more thing before I go" comment (reference to an old TV detective from the early 70's who was famous for this line before he finished talking with suspects). I paused on the way out of his office, turned back to him and sought clarification on two key resource points: money and people. I reminded him that the plan I proposed had a specific recommendation for financial and headcount "investments."

He quickly got to his point. He told me that I would receive no money or people resources for the project but that I should work with the President of the North American Pharmaceutical business to secure the appropriate support from his people. Swell! That's the ringing endorsement I was looking for (can you feel the sarcasm dripping from my last statement?). Again, a random movie reference popped into my head. Bill Murray from *Caddyshack* described his alleged experience as a golf caddy for the Dali Lama. After the round Bill asks him, "How about a little something for the effort?" The Dali replies, "Oh, there won't be any money, but when you die...on your death bed...you will receive total consciousness. Bill finished with the famous words, "So I got that going for me...which is nice."

Duly armed with my version of "total consciousness" from the boss man himself, I went to the pharmaceutical leadership, and then the brand teams and their supporting e-marketing people and let them know about this terrific opportunity to drive sales.

The pharmaceutical marketing team was thrilled to hear that the CEO of the company wanted them to support this new e-marketing effort and provide me with all of the support required. That was the gist of it.

How do you think that went over with the disenfranchised players in the pharmaceutical marketing organization? They just *loved* the fact that the *head of IT* from the *consumer* division was telling them how to do their jobs! And how do you think the pharmaceutical e-marketing and analytics teams felt about this initiative? In short, let's just say that this program, which had yet to be initiated officially, had already been gashed with one thousand paper cuts in an effort to stop the project in its tracks. One famous Monty Python line kept coming to my mind over and over again as the bloodletting through paper cuts continued. Two Monty Python characters were fighting in a sword duel. The lesser of the two had both arms cut off in the battle. The apparent victor declared the fight to be over, while the armless man proudly proclaimed, "It's just a flesh wound!" That was me... ready to continue fighting despite the lack of arms.

The reception to this idea (and the messenger) was chilly at best. Even the marketing team for the brand we were going to support wanted no part of the "dinner I was serving." The fact that there was an opportunity to drive customer behavior through more efficient and effective means was a secondary consideration. The more pressing consideration in the eyes of the brand team was who was telling whom to do what! The North American Pharmaceutical marketing team (including their close ally in commercial analytics) wanted nothing to do with a pilot of any sort...particularly one that came from an IT guy in the consumer division. Even the brand team for the selected marketing "experiment"—Zantac Syrup—which had a lot to gain since they would finally have some investment to drive their business—was apparently drinking the same kool-aid that the rest of the commercial folks were. They had little interest in a project that, for the first time in years, was geared towards driving customers to have the right conversation with their doctors about infant Gastroesophogeal Reflux Disease (GERD) which was the condition that Zantac Syrup treats. I felt like I had dragged the horse to water, splashed water in its face, but the horse refused to drink.

In order for innovation to occur, the champion needs to create an environment where there is no option but to succeed. Resistance is not a reason to stop... it is affirmation of the need to continue. The fact that there was universal and passionate resistance to the mere consideration of conducting a pilot program on non-essential brands meant that I must have been onto something. Remember my discussion about the Physics of Innovation? The bigger the impact and the faster you move, the more resistance you create. There was potential for big impact and there was speed...so, quite naturally, there was resistance....a lot of it! I used the resistance as a clear indicator that I must be onto something big and worthwhile.

As far as I was concerned, I had the "support" (at least verbally) of the CEO of the company to execute this program and I was going to get it done one way or the other! Failure was not an option. As I often say when things do not go as planned, "There is no such thing as bad news, just new information." And believe me, I got a lot of "new information" every day at GSK.

Despite my rosy outlook about the prospects of success, there were many among the GSK pharmaceutical team who were quite skilled at identifying reasons why this project would fail— and they put up an impassioned plea to kill this program before it saw the light of day. They tried a number of stall and kill tactics, including: this is not a priority brand; analytics can't support the analysis; and we simply do not have the money.

None of the objections derailed the project, though they did manage to slow the project down which eventually hurt the momentum of the effort.

The consistency of rejection and negativity regarding this initiative made me wonder whether there was in fact a group called the "Just Say No" department. Or, at a minimum, there had been significant investment in training people to just say no. The most accomplished of these people could reject something without having the first idea about the opportunity or the upside potential for GSK.

Despite the multi-level attacks on the program, my core team persevered and managed to move forward with the program in large part because I would not let it die. The key role that I had to play for the team was the champion. Despite the significant negativity and doubt surrounding the project at every step of the way, I had to continually ask my team members to "suspend disbelief" to make it happen. I gave them permission to believe that we could do it, and did everything possible to extinguish the more overt attempts to subvert the initiative at all levels. The team deserved this sort of support as a reward for their exhaustive efforts to get the program up and running in the face of so many obstacles. It was the least I could do.

The program we developed was designed to help mothers determine whether their infants suffered from infant GERD. There was a significant gap between the number of infants who suffer from GERD and the number of infants who are treated. The idea was to get mom's to visit the website, review GERD symptoms, print out the results, and then discuss the results with their physician to determine if the symptoms were related to infant GERD. The results clearly indicated that there was a big uplift in prescriptions for Zantac during the period when the on-line program was running. And a follow-up survey confirmed that mothers who came to the website and went through the symptom analyzer talked to their physicians and had prescriptions filled.

Oh, and along the way, we also realized a number of "collateral benefits" (which are unintended positive outcomes from your focus on overcoming organizational obstacles to innovation). Our click through rate was significantly better than the GSK average, and our cost per click was significantly lower than the GSK average. Despite these positive achievements, I was not "feeling the love" in the organization. Quite to the contrary, the more apparent success we showed, the more annoyed the resistors became. They appeared to be concerned that our results would raise questions as to why they had been unable to achieve similar results all along. In short, success could make them look bad.

With a stream of seemingly indisputable metrics, you may be wondering how the organization could not get behind this effort more profoundly? Well, let's just say that the corporate antibodies were out in full force trying to eliminate the foreign matter. The tool of choice for "elimination" was statistical mumbo-jumbo. The pharmaceutical commercial analytics team responsible for ensuring appropriate tracking and measurement of success and delivering a final report on the program seemed to make the actual results indecipherable. They were not happy about being forced to participate in a pilot that they did not initiate. Since they could not stop the program from happening, they did their best to minimize the impact of the pilot. It was a "testy" partnership to be sure.

One of the clear lessons I learned from the "support" we received from our commercial analytics partners was that I needed to do more to give them a reason to support the program. In an effort to get our analytics partner to support the initiative, I abdicated too much control over the final report to them without giving them enough reason to support the program.  As a result, the final report of the program under-represented the achievements associated with this initiative.

Because of my failure to carry this experiment through the "home stretch," we had a success that was dressed up as a failure by those people who felt like this project had been imposed upon them.  There was enough positive result from the program for us to proceed with another pilot program, but there was even less energy behind the second effort.  In essence, we lost the battle (and the war) because we were not able to move fast enough and maintain the momentum from the success of the initial pilot program.  I did a good job of getting top-down support from the CEO, but I failed to enroll the other players who would be critical to the success of the program.  To be effective at driving innovation, you need to be able to enroll supporters throughout the organization—not just those at the top.

### Lessons learned from *The "Top-Down" Approach Isn't Always Best*

⊙ **Be careful about the top-down approach.**  Support "from the top" helps motivate those willing to drive change and mobilizes resistance from the defenders of the status quo.  It would have been far better had I tried to enroll some of the players into the process before engaging the CEO for his support.

⊙ **Gain the trust of those clearly benefiting from your success.**  I should have done more work to get the brand team, analytics team, and the entire pharmaceutical marketing team in a position to win.  From the beginning they felt like this was something that was imposed on them, and that any success would be mine, not theirs. Had I done a better job enrolling the analytics team early in the process, they could have helped create a stronger team that all pulled in the same direction.

⊙ **The sirens song of the status quo is hard to overcome.** Big companies claim to want new and better ways, but few can resist the comfort of the status quo and the infrastructure built to maintain it. It is like the sirens song that caused sailors in ancient Greece to crash their ships into the rocky shoals (referenced in Homer's *Odyssey*). It sounds so right to stay the course, but eventually you crash!

⊙ **Surprises—even good ones—cause stress and trigger resistance.** It came as a big surprise that the CEO had endorsed a pilot program on a "non-strategic" pharmaceutical brand. Despite the clear potential upside for the brand from renewed focus and investment, the brand team resisted.

⊙ **Vocal opponents represent the tip of the iceberg of organized resistance.** Passive aggressive resistance—like the ice below the surface—is always deeper and represents 90% of the opposition.

⊙ **Share the credit for success with as many people as possible**. Especially with those whose toes you may have inadvertently stepped on. I could have done a better job managing some of the key players on the pharmaceutical marketing and commercial analytics teams.

⊙ **Make sure that you agree and stick to the appropriate success metrics in advance.** Many successes can be masqueraded as failures if you do not hold true to the agreed upon success metrics.

⊙**Persevere**.  Despite all of the resistance that will occur if your idea is big enough and you are moving fast enough, you need to stand up for what you believe.  Leverage your passion for the initiative to overcome obstacles.

⊙**Just succeeding for the business (finding a better and more profitable way to work) is not enough.**  You have to pay attention to the people impacted by your effort, make them owners of the approach, and make them look good. Otherwise, you run the risk of a seemingly good opportunity failing because there is not the right support for it.

# 23 | You Can't Spend What You Don't Have

This story highlights an example of creating innovative, low-cost marketing approaches out of necessity. When you don't have financial resources you find a way to get things done without money. This brand could have done what many choose to do, which is to bemoan their lack of resources and to feel persecuted/handicapped by the lack of investment. Instead, this brand developed a low-cost, highly effective approach to marketing because it had to. Necessity is the mother of invention.

Flixonase, like many GSK brands in the U.K., did not have money to lavish on expensive marketing programs. We had to do things smarter and more cost effectively than our competitors. Are you sensing a recurring theme here? Good ideas and opportunities typically evolve out of a need for doing more with less money. When you have money, you tend to do stupid things like spend it on the same things you have always done. When you don't have money, you have to be smart. It forces you to think differently about how to approach influencing customers. Is it possible that having less money could make you more successful? In many cases, the answer is yes! "Smart" marketing really just means driving more activity for less money. To do this, it is always a good idea to target people who can influence large groups of your customers. What made this particular innovative e-marketing program so compelling was its simplicity (a common theme for innovation: simple beats better). We developed a very simple marketing communication to Pharmacists and Assistant Pharmacists.

In the case of Flixonase (a product for seasonal allergies), while consumers did not need a prescription, they did need the help of a pharmacist or assistant pharmacist as the product was kept "behind" the counter—meaning consumers could not get it without help from the pharmacist. So clearly, the pharmacist could play a critical "influence" role for our brand, but what would motivate them to play that role? We needed to understand more about the emotional drivers of their behavior.

We learned that pharmacists feel good about themselves when they feel like they are bringing value to their customers. If we could help them feel more valued by their customers then we would be in a position to motivate them to the specific action we wanted them to take. In this case, the action was for the pharmacist to pass along to their customers useful allergy-related information that we communicated to them. That would be a big win for them and for GSK. Armed with relevant category information from GSK, the pharmacists were able to provide timely allergy-related information to their customers.

Based on the pharmacist's insight we developed a text-messaging program to support the Flixonase brand. The program had three critical components delivered on different days of the week:

- ❖ Pollen forecast for the upcoming week by geography;
- ❖ Facts/myths about allergies;
- ❖ Quiz on key allergy facts, and winners awarded pens, mugs, etc.

Pharmacists and Assistant Pharmacists raved about the program as it helped them bring more value to their customers who were suffering from allergies. As a result, pharmacists were more conversant with and helpful to customers in the allergy category and they also were more predisposed to recommend Flixonase as the brand of choice to potential patients. The results of this highly targeted text-messaging program were outstanding. While the program was running, the overall allergy category was down slightly, yet Flixonase sales were up nearly 50%! This was a huge success and yet another example of what organizations can achieve through rapid experimentation around inexpensive, non-traditional marketing approaches. Again, we had to do things differently (and smarter) because we did not have the luxury of doing stupid things (the same things we had always done) with a lot of cash.

**Lessons learned from *You Can't Spend What You Don't Have***

⊙ **Scarce resources increase creativity.** The brand did not have enough money to advertise on TV, so it invested wisely in targeted areas of influence. This successful text-messaging program would not have come about if the brand had money to invest in more traditional forms of advertising and promotion.

⊙ **Necessity is the mother of invention**. There are no free passes in business. The brand could not simply complain and whine about not having financial resources to grow the business. They had to do more with less.

⊙ **Focus on the major influencers of your customer's behavior.** We used our understanding of what motivates pharmacists to develop a program for them to help promote our brand to consumers. We provided pharmacists with information that made them much more helpful to their customers who suffered from allergies. The pharmacists then became the heroes who helped customers who were seeking allergy-relief.

# 24 | Don't Be Afraid to Be Called a Fool

This story is a classic example of applying a business model designed for one environment to another. I saw the potential of applying a peer-to-peer selling model (based on my own experience selling beer to college students) to the GSK business. Most people thought I was crazy...or more politely, "a fool." But I believed there was something there. I also was able to persuade others to suspend disbelief long enough to get the initiative started. Who would have thought that my experience as a beer representative in college would serve as the foundation for a unique peer-to-peer selling model for a pharmaceutical company? There were three key ingredients to this innovation.

### Ingredient One: The College Experience—The Foundation of an Opportunity

When I was a freshman at Duke, I was fortunate enough to have a teacher's assistant (TA) in Economics who just happened to be the Anheuser Busch Marketing Representative on campus— which is just a fancy, cleaned-up, resume-worthy name for the "Bud rep." As soon as I discovered this fact, I made it my mission to be the next "Bud rep" on campus. I hounded my TA relentlessly about the possibility of me taking over for him when he graduated in the spring. Eventually, I wore him down and he recommended me to his boss at the local distributor. I was hired.

I know what you are thinking. "Now that is a really challenging job...selling beer to college students!" The drinking age had just changed to 19 my freshman year and then moved to 21 with everyone that was legal grandfathered in. That made for a sizeable market! I share that with you as I know the environment is completely different on college campuses today. Parties with 30 kegs are unfathomable these days, but occurred fairly regularly for big events on campus back in the day. I was paid essentially to be social, keep an active network, and make sure parties served Budweiser. I suppose this was an early version of a "social network." I had to stay connected with all of the campus leaders of living groups, sororities and fraternities each month so that when an event was being planned, they would plan to use Budweiser products at the event. Because of this role, I knew a ton of people on campus and it was pretty easy for me to influence my network.

In the scheme of the jobs in my career, it seemed to be rather insignificant, but I have to say, "What a great job!" Basically, I got paid to socialize, and to "try" to sell beer to students. Tough job, I know, but someone has to do it. The job "forced" me to stay in contact with all of the President's and Social Chairs for all of the on-campus living groups, clubs, fraternities and sororities. I was a fairly gregarious person and this suited me just fine. I was paid to be me! What a concept.

This concept of identifying on-campus leaders—with large social networks—and giving them the right training and motivation provided me with the peer-to-peer selling experience that would be the foundation for the opportunity at GSK.

## Ingredient Two: The GSK Interview Process—You Get What You Get

In order to understand why the Head of Information Technology (IT) for GSK's Consumer Healthcare division (that'd be me, by the way) would start and manage a 400-person selling network based on the "Bud rep" model, I need to remind you of the approach I took to the GSK interview process (discussed in Chapter 22). Quite simply, I was just being me. I did not pretend to be something I was not. I never purported to be an IT "wiz." I was always someone who would push the envelope and try new things. Technology provided a lot of fuel for creativity and I was very clear in the interview process that I fully intended to leverage technology to drive sales and marketing initiatives.

During the interview process, I remember a number of times with different interviewers where I told them that I was not the guy for the job as it was described. Truth be told, I was not interested in the job as it was described. I was interested in the job as it should be—a job that has a direct and measurable impact on the business. I felt a bit like Robert Redford's role in the *Candidate*—where he ran for office on a campaign of "I'm not the right guy for the job." As the interview cycle continued through its numerous iterations, I think the interviewers started to understand what I meant. They did not need someone to watch over the back office business processing functions within the Consumer division. They needed someone to provoke the organization into thinking and acting differently. They needed someone who would leverage technology to drive sales and marketing.

They became more intrigued with a new and different role for the Global Head of IT. I was hired with complete transparency about my desire and passion for leveraging technology to create new value. That's who I was. And that is who they got.

Now you have the two ingredients that served as the basic raw material for the upcoming innovation: my past experience in college combined with a clear articulation about my passion for leveraging technology to create "new" value. All that was missing was the third ingredient...the action to make it happen!

### Ingredient Three: Take Action—Apply College "Bud Rep" Experience to GSK

The path to innovation, as you would expect, was not without a few bumps. One of the early bumps had to do with the preconceived notions of what IT could do at GSK. In short, it was "speak only when spoken to." That was not going to fly with me, especially since my entrepreneurial spirit could never be pinned down inside any "box."

After I had some time under my belt in my latest role at GSK— running the Global IT organization for the Consumer Healthcare business—I started to spread my wings a bit. Within a very short period of time, I increased the scope of my job responsibilities by adding the Head of Global e-Marketing to my role. In fact, having built and managed an internet business, I lived and learned more about the internet than anyone at GSK. Jack Ziegler, the President of GSK's Consumer Business, was not a technology maven, but he was a very sharp, forward-thinking leader. He recognized that I may have some skills that did not fit neatly into an IT "box." This is why he allowed me to take over the e-marketing responsibilities for his business. This move, as expected, provoked the aforementioned corporate antibodies (see Chapter 2).

Anyone that was in marketing or sales was deeply offended by the thought of an "IT guy" running e-marketing. It really did not matter that I had significant first-hand experience in the space. People could not imagine an "IT" person being in charge of e-marketing. It was actually quite comical from my perspective. If I had not been the Head of Global Information Technology and I had gotten the job as Head of Global e-Marketing, I don't think anyone would have had a problem with it. By virtue of my resume—extensive experience in marketing and the internet—I would have been very qualified for the job. Somehow, my connection to IT had muddied the waters and diluted my qualifications. They could not see past their own traditional preconceptions about what IT is and can do.

I guess in some ways, my "IT-ness" was a sort of ethnic class, and I can legitimately say that I experienced a bit of what I will term IT "stereotyping." I was the misunderstood minority who just happened to have experience and success in the world of technology and business. Still, many people could not get past some of these sweeping generalities (at least at that time) about IT folks:

- introverts
- work only in the dark
- can't speak the language (of business)
- can solve any computer or projector problem in any conference room or office
- speak only when spoken to
- not a marketing bone in their body
- love Dungeons and Dragons (an early predecessor of *Call of Duty*)

To some degree, I was able to overcome these perceptual obstacles because I was a bit tone deaf to the noise. I did not hear—more accurately, I chose not to listen to—the panicked cries from marketers who were more concerned about who was orchestrating things than the value being created for the business. My tone deafness served me well. And it was an important lesson in innovation. In order to get things done, you really need to listen to those around you. But, and this is an important "but," you also need to recognize that value-creating innovation looks and sounds like folly to others until the moment it becomes "genius." Resistance is a natural part of the process of creating new value. When you face resistance, you need to identify the "gems" of learning that can help improve your innovation and keep driving. Don't let resistance deter you from your goal.

The "innovator" trapped inside my "IT" body helped change the perception about what IT can do for the business. The innovator inside quite enjoyed applying experiences from one part of my life and career to a new situation. Often times, the juxtaposition of an old experience with a modern problem/challenge can lead to really cool, new value creation. There may not be an obvious connection at first, but you need to try to determine if there is new value that can be created.

I applied the "Bud rep" model to develop a fairly innovative viral selling organization for the over-the-counter and pharmaceutical products that GSK sold. The concept was simple, at least in my mind: create a network of student ambassadors who were appropriately motivated to persuade their friends to purchase GSK OTC brands. Studies had shown that lifetime purchase behaviors are formed at this critical juncture when "kids" are making purchase decisions for the first time without the direct influence of their parents. If I could influence their choice of beer, I figured, I could influence their choice of drug! Now, now, it's not what you think. I meant to say that if you can sell beer to college students, you can sell drugs to them. Wait, that's not it either. I think you get the point. We were really trying to sell OTC products and later train the student representatives to do disease state awareness campaigns among their peers for prescription products.

My belief was that the same model that worked in college—having students selling beer to other students a primitive form of "peer-to-peer" selling—could work at GlaxoSmithKline.

Rather than have the students sell beer, we would have them promote our OTC brands like Aquafresh, Sensodyne, and Nicorette (smoking control) to their classmates. Once we proved that this model worked for OTC brands then we could explore the potential of leveraging this viral network to support our prescription brands with disease state awareness programs on campuses.

You can imagine how enthusiastically this idea was received in a very conservative pharmaceutical company. People looked at me like I had two heads. And once I explained that the model for this "opportunity" was the Bud rep job I had in college, then people looked at me as if I had three heads.

This leads me to one of the many critically important lessons in value creation, innovation and entrepreneurship: you must be able to "suspend disbelief." In order to unleash the talents of people who would otherwise be paralyzed by their own doubts about the viability of an initiative, it is important that you ask them to "suspend disbelief." First, acknowledge that there may be some legitimate reasons why the project could fail—this is the disbelief part of the equation. Then ask people to suspend the disbelief in order to focus on the ways that it can be done. For your part, you need to be the one giving people "permission to believe" that the project or opportunity can be done. You cannot have any weak moments as your team will be looking for signs of weakness. Even if you have doubts, you cannot reveal any. When they look at you, all they should see is the belief that it will happen—even if you don't know exactly how.

As I now try to explain the rationale behind the origin of this peer-to-peer selling model, it seems a bit flimsy. Maybe I am beginning to understand the obstacles people raised in a new light. Most good innovations start out that way—not fully baked, a little flimsy. You need to give them further shape and form and the only way to do that is by doing something—not thinking about it, or analyzing it to death. Action precipitates innovation. The real opportunity evolved out of the concept of leveraging a motivated connected network. That's what the Bud rep job allowed me to do—establish a connected network of on-campus leaders. It was viral marketing long before there was something as convenient as the internet to accelerate the spreading of the virus.

So the big leap (or "hypothesis" in innovation-speak) was whether we could build a network of connected leaders on campuses around the U.S. and motivate them to sell GSK over-the-counter products to their peers. While I confess that I had some concern that the appeal of GSK OTC brands would not be as great as beer, I had already "suspended my disbelief" in order to progress the experiment. This was a classic "peer-to-peer" selling model. Such a simple hypothesis should be easy to test...or so I thought.

The plan was as follows:

1. Identify and hire on-campus influencers—people who are already recognized/established as "connected" individuals.
2. Pay a small monthly stipend to all students—but not large enough to attract people who are only in it for the money. We wanted the individuals who were motivated by the opportunity to leverage their personal networks.
3. Develop incentive program to motivate the best performers. We wanted to offer a significant incentive for the top performers in the hope that it would drive creative promotional activity that we had not anticipated.
4. Build a marketing portal to monitor promotional activity.
5. Create uniquely identifiable coupons to track individual performance.
6. Gain support from interested GSK OTC brands and clear medical/legal/regulatory hurdles.

This may be an oversimplification of the plan as each part of the plan had a fair amount of complexity associated with it... but you get the idea.

The first major hurdle we had to clear was the hiring process to build our network of influencers. We planned to hire 40 student representatives at 20 universities around the country. We had a small budget for the "experiment" so we needed to spend our money wisely. I sought out the expert advice of the GSK Human Resources (HR) department. HR can be a valuable partner to help drive meaningful business value when you involve them early in the solution. No, really!

Initially, HR wanted us to conform to the well-established policies and procedures in place for hiring new employees. If we had adopted those standards for hiring our student "ambassadors" (as we liked to call them) it would have been cost-prohibitive. We had to do things differently...we had to start small and act differently...like a start-up with limited resources. There may have been a little persuasion, encouragement, cajoling, and force applied in order to do what we needed to do, but we got there together.

Our plan was to scan university databases—publicly available information only—to identify on-campus leaders, e.g. President's or Social Chair's of on-campus living groups or organizations. We then planned to send a direct message (e-mail) to let them know that we would like them to be a part of this special new program that GSK was initiating. Those interested would then go through a few phone interviews and the folks that we liked would be offered a job. Sounded like a very tight, efficient, and cost-effective approach.

Our HR partners had their own view of what needed to be done. They wanted to seek out candidates in the tried and true methods of the past: pay for an advertisement in the student newspaper to generate interest, screen the resumes and then interview the candidates. They also wanted to be sure that we were paying the representatives a fair rate for our estimate of the time required to plan and execute promotional activities. Oh, yeah, and HR insisted that we interview each of the candidates face-to-face as that has always been the way it was done. The airfare costs associated with their suggested plan would have exhausted our entire budget and would leave us with no money to pay the students or to build the website. That's a bit of a problem. We were at an impasse. What to do?

Fortunately, there was one very forward-looking HR professional, Lou Manzi, who coincidentally was the first person to hire me out of undergraduate—so he must have REALLY been forward looking! I explained to him what we were trying to do, and he cleared the path for us to proceed with our "new method" of recruiting and provided valuable support as the program progressed. He was one of those rare individuals who started with "why" you were doing something instead of "what" you plan to do. This is a good reminder of the importance of staying in touch with your network (see Chapter 5). There were still a number of HR professionals who were upset that we were not following the standard process and they made sure to let us know repeatedly, that they would not take responsibility for the quality of the individuals we hired. I was totally comfortable with their distance and welcomed the challenge of finding great talent. As long as they were not standing in our way, I was confident we would succeed.

Why spend so much time talking about a seemingly meaningless obstacle raised by a support function? I'll tell you why: collateral benefits. Collateral benefits are benefits that are discovered on the path to success. They are not specific areas of focus for the original objective, but benefits that result from overcoming obstacles that stand in the way of success. HR was kind enough to raise significant objections to our "alien" hiring process and rightfully pointed out that it was vastly different than the existing process.  What we created in the end was a process, built out of the necessity for a lower cost solution, that was vastly superior to the old process in every conceivable way.  It cost less, took less time, and identified higher quality talent.  Not a bad trifecta!

As a testament to the quality of the representatives we hired, after the first year of the Campus Consumers program, GSK hired 35% of the students for full-time employment.  Considering that GSK did not typically hire undergraduates at all, this was a big deal.  One of those hires (Ajay Kori) within two years of his hire was recognized by the CEO of GSK for his significant contributions to building an internal social network of new hires.

The "alien" process that HR had initially found so objectionable became the only way that GSK hires graduate students and undergraduates out of universities in the U.S. and the U.K.  The quality of the candidates and the significant cost-savings generated was simply too much for HR to ignore.  They adopted this approach as their own.  Not a bad outcome…but totally not the focus of what we were setting out to do.  It just happened on the path to success. This was a true collateral benefit.  We did not set out with the goal of developing a new hiring process that yielded top candidates while saving the company millions of dollars in costs, but it happened as a result of our need to overcome an obstacle that stood in the path to success.  One of the key lessons:  Don't accept the way things are done because they have always been done that way.  This is yet another example where scarce resources (limited or no budget) were great source of innovation.

Once we cleared the HR obstacles around recruiting, we saw plenty more hurdles to clear from many different parts of the organization.  It felt good to get some momentum by moving past this first one. It reminded me of another random movie quote. "We mock what we don't understand," Dan Akroyd said in *Spies like Us*. This quote was particularly relevant as people who did not understand what we were trying to accomplish with the Campus Consumer program "mocked" it. There were many detractors dispersed evenly across the business.

One detractor cleverly disguised himself as a proponent for a little while. He was one of the sales leaders for the consumer division and he seemed to be "intrigued" at the prospect of creating a sales force at universities. I put quotation marks around "intrigued" for a reason. He wanted to make sure that he was aware of everything we were planning to do since our success had the potential to make what his current team was doing look bad by comparison. Does that sound strange? People in the organization were actually more concerned about not looking badly than winning in the market place. They feigned interest in and support for this program for the purpose of learning enough to kill the program. While this sounds incredibly cynical, it is the truth.

I recall a conversation that we had with the core group responsible for driving the effort. The sales leader participated in the teleconference, and decided that this meeting was the appropriate forum to launch his first SCUD missile at the project. He targeted the financial assumptions underlying approval of the project. Keep in mind, the project had already been approved and funded by the President of the Consumer business. My antagonist's question was a simple one, "What was your assumption on the redemption rate for coupons distributed by the students?" I informed him that our model assumed a 20% redemption rate. Well you would have thought that we had just landed in the audience of a comedy club with all of the laughter heard on that call—mostly his laughter. He asked condescendingly, "Do you have any idea what the coupon redemption rate is for our Free Standing Inserts (FSI's) in Sunday circulars?" I quickly replied, "In fact, I do. Typically, redemption rates are in the 0.5-1.0% range." His laughter suddenly stopped and he shifted to concern. He suspected that I might know a little more about the business than he had assumed. Still, he continued his interrogation, "If you know those redemption numbers, what makes you think that you could get a 20x higher redemption rate with your program?" Again, I did not hesitate. "This program is entirely different. It is driven by connected individuals reaching out to the friends and classmates and encouraging them to use the coupon to purchase the relevant GSK brands." In this case, you have a friend asking a friend to do them a favor. The message from our Campus ambassadors to their network of friends was simple: "Buy the product you need to buy anyway, use the coupon when you do, and put me in a better chance to win $10K in the competition for the highest number of redemptions." We thought it was compelling enough to drive a significantly higher redemption rate. As it turned out, we were almost exactly right. The redemption rate at the end of the first year of the program was 21%. We missed it by 1%. But, to be clear, we underestimated the rate by 1%. My bad.

I could have "caved" in this discussion, but as is true with most innovators who are doing new things, you need to believe in your opportunity in the face of skeptics, resistors and critics. I believed that my assumptions had solid rationale and were a better indicator of how thing would turn out than the stats on a completely unrelated and impersonal way of distributing coupons to consumers. In our case, the "personal touch" was worth an incremental 20 percentage points. I'd like to say that there was a scientific method that I used to crank out this number, but there was not. I felt like it was a reasonable assumption if we were able to hire the high-caliber connected individuals we were seeking.

On the heels of a pretty significant success in our first year—

where we drove millions of dollars in incremental sales at a fraction of the cost, we doubled the size of the network for year two—80 representatives at 40 universities. Additionally, some of the brands that had lukewarm interest in participating suddenly became much more interested—most notably the Nicorette brand (nicotine replacement therapy). We drove huge incremental sales through our program. It was getting harder and harder to "explain away" or "dismiss" the impact that we were having on the business. That said, there were still some stalwarts who were sticking closely to the company line that this program was too expensive and drove too little impact (despite revenues 6-7x cost) to continue.

The bigger "problem" that I had was that it was a "nice-to-have" program that generated incremental millions for the business, but it was not big enough. Only if I could demonstrate impact at a much higher level, would I be able to get the sustained attention of the GSK Executive Leadership Team. The solution—to me—was simple. Scale this program up significantly and support the much more profitable GSK pharmaceutical brands. This would move the decimal point over a few spots on the financial upside. That should do the trick!

We looked at a couple of brands that had a clear opportunity based on the fact that our "network of influencers" was particularly strong for women 18-24 years of age. GSK was expecting approval for its cervical cancer vaccine—Cervarix. This was a particularly difficult segment to reach through traditional media, but we had the perfect solution for them. This was the big opportunity we were looking for. I reached out to the Cervarix team and gained their support for funding the increase in the size of the network from 80 representatives to 400 while also expanding the university "footprint" from 40 to 200 universities. This was a significant ramp up in the scope and scale of the program.

One of the critical first steps I took was to identify some of the biggest internal obstacles to the success of this effort on the prescription side. I had to seek out "they." Who are "they" you may ask? "They" are the ones that won't let you do anything in a company. You usually hear it in the context of "they" will never let you do that here. In this case, not surprisingly, "they" turned out to be the legal team (affectionately known internally as the "just say no" department). Clearly, I had to have the legal folks supportive of what and how we were going to talk about the cervical cancer category as they needed to bless the messaging that we were going to create for the students. We knew that we could not do specific brand promotion, but felt It would be really important to do significant unbranded peer-to-peer disease awareness programs on campuses.

We met on numerous occasions with the head of legal for this brand and over successive meetings helped to evolve her thinking from "we can't do this," to "it would be irresponsible of us NOT to do this program." The key to her support was involving her early in the process. We needed to understand her concerns before trying to convince! After listening to her position, we made it clear that we were going to do something and that we wanted to make sure we did it in a way that she could support. In essence, we made her an indispensible part of the solution. We provided the clay for her to mold into a solution that worked for her. Here is an important lesson: Get close to the biggest obstacles early. Seek to understand the driver of their decisions as you try to help them understand the purpose behind yours.

We did not wait until we had invested significant time, energy and resource to get our program fully-baked, and then seek her approval of the completed masterpiece. If we had, I am certain we would have been rejected outright. Instead, we socialized the concept with the legal team, listened to their initial concerns and encouraged them to take an active role in helping us shape the program in a way that they could support. The legal team became an essential partner in "co-creating" this solution. Nobody at GSK worked with legal that way. Our legal counterpart was incredibly insightful and helpful in getting us rolling in the right direction. Moreover, because she was so involved in shaping the program, she began to take a certain degree of ownership of the program itself and genuinely appreciated the way we engaged her.

As our team continued with our plans to support Cervarix, we heard a constant refrain from the naysayers around the organization: they will never let you do this, they will never let you do this. Just for kicks, I would ask them who the "they" was to whom they refer. Naturally, they would say that it is legal—who, unbeknownst to them, we had been working with from the start of this project. I would then ask them rhetorically, "Oh you mean the legal person who is presenting the "do's and don'ts" to these 400 student representatives in Salt Lake City? You mean that legal person? I'm pretty sure she is on-board." Our legal person was great. She did an outstanding job outlining the parameters that all of the students had to use as their guide for promotional activity.

There was a very interesting external development as we were ramping up for our third year of the campus program. Imitation is the sincerest form of flattery…shortly after the conclusion of our second year we began to hear from our students that Merck recruiters had taken a lot of interest in the Campus Consumer program. In the fall of 2007, Merck experimented with a similar concept on campuses for its own cervical cancer vaccine, Gardasil. They launched a university-focused disease awareness campaign led by (drum roll please) on-campus student ambassadors! This is Merck—the most ultraconservative of all pharmaceutical companies. I guess we were on to something if they found a way to test a similar concept as well.

Changes in leadership can take a lot of wind out of the sails (and in this case, "sales") of a program. One of the keys to the early success of the program was the support of my two bosses—Jack Ziegler, President of Consumer Healthcare, and Ford Calhoun, Chief Information Officer for GSK. They supported the original experiment, accepted that there would be learning along the way, and that the ultimate success would evolve out of this learning. Unfortunately for the program (and me), both Jack and Ford retired within a year of one another. Their successors brought their own views of what the focus of their "IT" resources should be. Let's just say it was a more narrow and traditional view of IT—an organization that takes orders, follows directions, and does not push the boundaries to develop new solutions. Did I mention that following orders is not really my forte?

The new President of the Consumer Healthcare division was interested in making his own mark on the business and, not surprisingly, he was not particularly interested in continuing to build on programs that were part of his predecessor's legacy. Continued success and increased visibility of the Campus Consumer program became almost like a thorn in the new President's side. He had little interest in learning more about the program and how it could be leveraged to create new selling networks for the business as he was focused on his own business initiatives.

Sensing that future support of the program may be in jeopardy due to the changes in leadership, I sought out new allies on the pharmaceutical side of the business. Since we were in line to support a few of the pharmaceutical brands—including one of GSK's biggest new launches in years—and since the pharmaceutical side of the business was picking up the majority of operating costs for the program—the Consumer business was not in a position to oppose the programs continued progress.

But, in the summer of 2006, GSK's world changed. One of the company's biggest pharmaceutical brands came under huge scrutiny by the FDA as negative publicity circulated about the safety profile of the product. GSK looked bad, the FDA looked bad, and the relations between the two got dramatically worse. Because of this souring relationship, the FDA was taking a much longer and harder look at approvals for GSK brands—including the impending approval of Cervarix—the cervical cancer vaccine that we were preparing to support. The expected approval date kept getting pushed back further and further and into the fall of 2007, it looked like we would not have any cervical cancer promotional activity to do at all.

Without a guarantee of support from our newfound friends on the pharmaceutical side due to their preoccupation with far more important FDA-related issues, the fate of the program was left to discretionary funding from the Consumer and IT side. My two new bosses elected to cancel funding for the program. The brilliant idea—a viral peer-to-peer marketing selling force on campuses around the country, which had been painstakingly built over the past three years—had officially been extinguished. The 400 student representatives who had already been trained and were conducting promotions around the country were informed that the program was coming to end in December 2007. What a waste. The power that this network had to influence the future was immense, but GSK no longer had an interest in it.

You might ask why executives who purport to be interested in driving innovation would pull the plug on a program that had the potential to evolve into a much more powerful social network at the dawn of the social networking age. That would be a good question. As best as I can figure, it really came down to priorities. Success of this program would always be attributed to the original visionaries who helped fund it. The new consumer President had his own priorities and had no attachment to this program as there was no specific upside for him—making it a very low priority.

The mistake I made was that I did not do more to try to make it more of a priority or something that fits with one of his stated priorities for the business. I could have done more to try to enroll him into the potential of this program rather than seek other partners who would serve as a counter-balance for his disinterest. I should have relentlessly engaged him to ensure that he understood the potential upside for the business— under his watch. That said, there was definitely a part of me that wanted no part in begging the President to reconsider. I suppose this is where I let my ego get the better of me. I felt like I had proven that the program had value and could have even more value in the future. My boss had little interest in hearing anything about it. I let my own pride prevent me from taking the necessary steps to try to get him on board with the program. Shame on me!

Admittedly, the way that the program quickly unraveled had left a bad taste in my mouth and took away some of the normal zest I had for my role at GSK. It was on the heels of the program's transition from a highly innovative engine of new sales generation to a program that could not be supported that I realized it was time for me to leave. Again, my thoughts drifted back to "grasshopper" from the old *Kung Fu* weekly series on TV. The blind sage holding pebbles in his hand and saying to the young grasshopper, "When you can snatch these pebbles from my hand, it will be time for you to leave." I felt like I had just snatched the pebbles. I needed to unleash my innovative energies outside the confines of GSK. I needed to recharge my batteries and get back on the value creation train.

Fortunately for me, the company was about to undergo a serious restructuring of the entire organization. I was able to secure a favorable "release" from GSK. Translation: I had some paid time off to figure out what my next step would be. Although I think the company wanted to keep me on board and continue to pursue innovative approaches to generating new value for GSK, I was convinced that they would not be able to do their part. As my new IT boss said at the time, "It is the nail that sticks up that gets the hammer." I was certainly the nail and I definitely felt the constant barrage of hammers on my head for six years. In any event, it all was a blessing for me as I really took advantage of that time off to network and to set the course for what I am doing today—running an innovation and marketing services consultancy.

Additionally, during my transition to my next business opportunity, I was able to spend real quality time with my 3-year-old daughter—Brynn. I had not had a similar opportunity with any of my other children at that age, so it was a real treasure for me.

⊙ ⊙ ⊙

### Lessons learned from *Don't Be Afraid to Be Called a Fool*

⊙ **Apply experiences from one area to another.** Who would have thought that the "Bud rep" job I had in college would be the source of such a cool viral marketing program at a pharmaceutical company? Good things happen when you try to force seemingly unrelated things together.

⊙ **Don't be afraid to be called a fool.** You need to have thick skin if you are going to drive new initiatives in organizations. All great innovations are foolish until the moment they succeed. If I had a nickel for every time someone called me a fool, I could have funded this entire program myself!

⊙ **Suspend disbelief.** You need to acknowledge to your team that there are many ways that something cannot be done. Then you need to ask your team to "suspend disbelief" and focus on the way things can be done.

⊙ **Beware of the silent resistance.** I have come to appreciate the vocal opposition. While sometimes painful to hear, it may actually speed the pace of your learning and progress. Silent resistance, aka passive aggressive behavior, is far more dangerous—and sinister—as apparent "support" can disappear without notice or reason.

⊙ **Understand the naysayers before trying to convince.** By listening to the concerns of the opposition you can better understand how you can navigate around and through the objections.

⊙ **Get close to your opposition early in the process.** In this case, legal was clearly going to be the biggest obstacle to the expansion of the program's purview into pharmaceuticals. I approached one of the legal head's in the pharmaceutical business and let her know what we planned to do on campuses, and revealed to her that we were counting on her to help us figure out how we can do it in in a way she could support.

⊙ **Co-create a solution.** By allowing people to participate in shaping the ultimate solution, we created a number of internal "ambassadors" who evangelized the merits of the program. We did not need, nor did we want absolute control and credit. If you share both, you get results!

⊙ **Celebrate collateral benefits.** We had no intention of creating a new recruiting process at universities, but that is one of the side-benefits that was generated from our work. We celebrated that win as it saved the company millions in recruiting costs.

⊙ **Re-embrace leadership who can help or hinder your initiatives**. I did not do a very good job of selling the merits of the Campus Consumer program to my new boss. I knew he was not sold on the concept initially. Rather than spending the time to convince him of the program's merits, I sought to insulate the project from his control. That was a mistake.

⊙ **"Do your homework."** It was important that I understood the FSI response rate or my credibility might have been hurt with the other team members. When you're trying to innovate, resistors will try to portray you as someone who is out of touch with reality. Knowing all the details and doing all of your homework is important to make sure others aren't convinced you are out of touch.

⊙ **A champion needs to stand by the mission and protect it (and the team) in the face of all enemies—foreign and domestic!** Whether the obstacles are internal or external, the champion needs to fight on until the mission is accomplished.

# 25 | Quality, Not Quantity, Matters Most

I had the opportunity at GSK to attend a very worthwhile executive training session. The course was a week long and attracted leaders from all over the globe. This was a huge commitment that GSK made to the development of its senior most leaders in recognition of the importance of the "soft" skills of management. There was a lot of work done leading up to and during the week long session to identify your personal style, strengths and weaknesses. Self-awareness is a critical building block for success and this program was designed to make executives more self-aware. It was a very reflective week.

The culmination of the session was particularly memorable. After being turned inside out all week to discover everything you knew but never really wanted to admit about yourself, finally there was a competition! All of the participants were seated in the audience—auditorium style. The proctors asked for two volunteers to participate in a small competition. I quickly raised my hand, squirmed and did everything to get noticed in the hope that they would pick me to compete. Did I mention that I have a bit of a competitive streak? Anyway, unfortunately for me, I was not selected. All was not lost however, as the competition taught me some valuable lessons.

The two participants—maybe competitors or "warriors" would be more accurate—strode to the front of the room and awaited their instruction. There were two tables in front of the competitors with some sort of bulk hidden beneath a cotton sheet. The main proctor pulled back the two sheets and revealed a large pile of poker chips on each table. He then explained that the object of the competition was to get as many points as possible in 10 seconds and that the chips represented points. Without much more advance notice, the proctor said, "Ready, set, go." The scramble was on. One of the competitors was grabbing handfuls and trying to stuff his pockets. The other competitor came up with a better plan and un-tucked his shirt and started scooping the chips from the table into his shirt which was now doubling as a sack. Soon the 10 seconds were up and it was clear that the man with the "shirt move" had collected significantly more chips. The first competitor argued unsuccessfully that the person who used the shirt move was cheating. He complained that nobody had told him that he could do that. Then again, nobody told him he could not (lesson here for those innovators in the audience: don't wait for someone to give you permission). The shirt sack competitor clearly had a significantly higher number of chips and had apparently won the competition. But not so fast...

After the mad grasp for the chips ended, the proctor provided some new information to the competitors. All chips were not worth the same amount. You could hear mumbling and grumbling from the audience and a hopeful look from competitor number one. The proctor went on to say that the point value was as follows: white chips (of which there were many) = 1 point; red chips (of which there were not that many) = 100 points; blue chips (of which there were very few) = 10,000 points.

A recalculation of the scoring led to an entirely different result. The competitor who thought he had lost had one blue chip. The shirt sack competitor had none. In short, the person who collected fewer chips but collected the right chip won.

Now what is the lesson in all of this? Focus on the really important, meaningful activities at work that drive value (blue chips). There are very few of these around and you cannot let yourself get derailed from your "blue chips" no matter how strong the resistance is. You need to hold onto them as a blue chip and make sure that you see the project through. What about the white chips? Well, white chips equate to the dozens of meetings you participate in each month that lead to no tangible result, no value generated. They are merely activities masquerading as productive behavior. The activities take up space, but they have very little real worth. You need to remain focused on your blue chip opportunities and do everything you can to minimize the number of white chips (low value activities) that you accumulate and stand in the way of your progress on the blue chip opportunities.

**Lessons learned from *Quality, Not Quantity, Matters Most***

⊙ **Focus on what matters most.** You must identify and make time for high-impact "blue chip" opportunities to channel your energy and passion.

⊙ **Clear your calendar of white chips to make time for blue chip "innovation."** Innovation takes time. You need to create the time by eliminating low value time drains.

⊙ **Being busy is not the same as being productive.** Eliminate as many of the low-value white chips from your day in order to make time for value-driving activities.

⊙ **Eliminate activities that take up time and don't contribute value.** Many meetings, reports and communications served a useful purpose at one point in time. As time moves on and the utility is gone, you must actively eliminate low- or no-value activities. Otherwise, your calendar gets clogged with white chip activities.

# 26 | Summary of Key Innovation Ideas and Concepts

What did you learn from your entertaining journey through *Diary of an Innovator: Finding the Path Not Taken*? I hope you learned enough to bring out the innovator inside you! Here are a number of the key lessons I hope you can incorporate into the fiber of your future innovation efforts:

1. **You can do anything you think you can...and only what you think you can...nothing more.** Innovation success depends on the power of belief. It may not be the first way you envisioned it, but if you believe, you will find the way.

2. **Suspend disbelief.** You need to capture all of the reasons why something cannot be done (this is the disbelief part) and then suspend that disbelief in order to focus on how you <u>can</u> get it done.

3. **Give people permission to believe in you and your idea.** People will look to you for permission to believe or for signs of weakness. If you don't believe, they won't believe. Their belief starts with you.

4. **The Physics of Innovation**.
   - Mass = Size of the impact or change
   - Velocity = Speed at which the impact/change occurs
   - The faster you move or the larger the impact/change, the more resistance you cause
   - If you are not getting resistance, your idea is not big enough or you are not moving fast enough

5.  **Innovation triggers the corporate antibodies**. Innovation causes change, change causes resistance, and the bigger the change and faster you move, the more resistance you create. Resistance is a natural reaction, not a sign that innovation cannot be achieved.

6.  **Classify your innovation as an "experiment."** Experiments are less threatening to the keepers of the status quo. Experiments never fail... they produce learning.

7.  **You can't drive down a highway using the rear-view mirror as your guide.** Looking backwards to drive forward does not work. It is a great way to get you back to where you were, but is not a particularly good way to get you where you want to go. The same is true with innovation...you must look forward to achieve your future.

8.  **Innovation: It's not what you "no..." it's what you know.** You can't drive innovation by rejecting opportunities and saying no, you need to try stuff in order to know how to succeed.

9.  **Hear "Know" instead of "No."** When someone tells you that you can't do something—or "No!" You need to assume that they simply don't "know" enough to say yes...yet. Take ownership and accountability for getting them to know. Just surround every no with a "k" and a "w" and <u>K</u>eep <u>W</u>orking!

10. **Innovate or Die.** If you give yourself an option to fail, you will. If your only option is success, you will use your failures as steps on the path to success.

11. **Nobody has the patience to wait for the future.** You need to move quickly, try things, adapt and create the future now.

12. **Don't let your experience blind you to opportunities**.
    The more experience and knowledge you accumulate, the
    less you see (in terms of opportunities). The less you see
    the less you do. There are always lots of reasons whey
    something cannot be done. Focus on the ways it can be
    done.

13. **Inexperience can be a great driver of innovation**. When
    you are not burdened by the reasons why things cannot be
    done, you focus on how it can be done.

14. **Tomorrow is perfection. Perfection is Tomorrow**. Ask
    yourself, when is it actually "tomorrow." Does it ever get
    here? You can get really close to tomorrow (milliseconds
    away just before midnight), but you never actually reach
    tomorrow. The same is true with achieving "perfect." You
    can get really, really close, but you can never get there.
    Don't wait for perfect. Take action today.

15. **Beware the sirens sweet song of the status quo.** It is
    perfectly normal to deny the validity of any possible solution
    that challenges the accepted standards of the status quo.
    Don't be normal.

16. **You can learn a lot from rejection.** Resistors see things
    that you do not. Listen to and work with them. By working
    closely with resistors, you can effectively plow the vast fields
    of corporate sameness and sow the seeds of innovation!

17. **There is no such thing as bad news…just new
    information.** You will constantly discover information that
    flies in the face of your original assumptions…this is just new
    information that will allow you to get on the path to success.
    Bad news is crippling, new information is the key ingredient
    to success.

18. **Cash is king.** Without money, you can't do anything. Spend money as late as possible and get it as soon as possible.

19. **Until the money is in the bank, the money is not in the bank.** A handshake and even a signed document does not mean that you have the money you need. You don't have any money until the money is actually in the bank (or in your possession).

20. **The less money you need, the more people are willing to invest.** If you appear desperate, you are. If you appear secure, you are. Investors would rather invest in secure than desperate businesses.

21. **When you have money, you do stupid things.** You have to have some money, but when you have too much there is a real risk that you will do stupid things—like spend it because you have it. When you don't have it, you find a way to accomplish your tasks without money. Be smart.

22. **When you don't have money, you do smart things...because you have to.** This is just a corollary of #18. The key is that you must find a way to accomplish your tasks without the "easy way out" of spending money to accomplish it. Necessity is the mother of invention. If you must get something done and you had no money, you would find a way to do it.

23. **Thinking isn't doing...doing is doing**. Thinking is a precursor to doing. Thinking without action has no value. It is the "doing" that creates value.

24. **Champions need to create an environment where there is no option but to succeed.** If you give yourself an option, you will not fight as hard to succeed in the face of

resistance, obstacles and challenges...because...you have an option. Don't give yourself an option.

25. **Don't be afraid to be called a fool!** All great innovations are foolish until the moment they succeed. Then they are genius!

26. **Get close to the biggest obstacles early.** Embrace those who may stand in your way and allow them to help you co-create your solution.

27. **Inexperience is a great source of inspiration for innovation.** The more you know, the less you see...the less you see, the less you do. Don't let your experience limit you. Take advantage of your inexperience!

# ABOUT THE AUTHOR

Tom combines a unique blend of strategy, marketing, general management, technology and Internet experience along with his entrepreneurial passion for creating new business models. He is currently President and CEO of Omega Group and the Founder and CEO of a new marketing and innovation consultancy, TB Innovative. Visit **www.tbinnovative.com**.

Tom has started a number of businesses in the U.S. and around the globe and has a long history of successfully driving innovative sales and marketing programs from his 25+ years at J&J, GSK, P&G and a number of entrepreneurial business ventures.

He helped establish and build new international business ventures between Janssen Pharmaceuticals and Johnson & Johnson Consumer Products. He launched more than 25 brands in five different countries – and served on the Board of Directors of two international business units.

Tom spent 6 years as Head of Global Information Technology and eMarketing for GlaxoSmithKline Consumer Healthcare.

Tom was the co-founder and CEO of OmniChoice—an Internet business that sold decision support software to telecom, cable, and utility providers. He also worked as VP of Sales and Marketing for Intermedia—an Internet agency.

Tom holds a B.A. degree in Economics from Duke University and he earned his MBA in Entrepreneurial Management and Marketing from the Wharton School of Business. He is an Adjunct Professor teaching *First Steps to Starting a New Business* at Wharton's Small Business Development Center and teaches *Entrepreneurial Marketing* at Villanova's School of Business. Tom also provides executive coaching to a number of clients.

In his spare time, Tom enjoys spending time with his wife and four kids who remind him everyday of the possibilities of what can be.

57616R00137

Made in the USA
Charleston, SC
08 October 2013